D0992517

Advance Praise for

The Purpose Factor

"What is the difference between success and failure? Having a purpose. Brian and Gabrielle Bosché show us this clearly in The Purpose Factor. The Purpose Factor *unlocks the keys to living a successful and purposeful life."*

—**Dwayne "The Rock" Johnson**, Hollywood Actor

"The secret to success is good leadership, and good leadership is all about making the lives of others better. This should be your purpose daily. The purpose that defines you and drives you. The Purpose Factor *lays out how to find your purpose and let it lead you to success."*

—**Tony Dungy**, Pro Football Hall of Fame NFL Coach

"Many fail in life because they have been unable to achieve singleness of purpose. Purpose is what determines success both personally and professionally. Without purpose there is no success. Brian and Gabrielle Bosché understand this and have written The Purpose Factor *so everyone can discover what their purpose is and achieve the success they desire."*

—**Gary Keller**, *NYT* Bestselling Author
of *The ONE Thing* and Founder of Keller Williams Realty

"Get clear on what you want. If you don't have a purpose, you won't succeed. Determine your purpose in The Purpose Factor. *Once you have identified your purpose, nothing will hold you back."*

—**Lewis Howes**, *NYT* Bestseller and Host
of The School of Greatness Podcast

"It isn't about the journey but the purpose of your journey that defines you. Brian and Gabrielle Bosché take us on a journey to find that purpose in The Purpose Factor.*"*

—**Rachel Hollis**, *NYT* Bestselling Author and CEO of The Hollis Co.

"You can do anything you set your mind to if you have a purpose. Your potential is limitless. Everything can be figured out. Brian and Gabrielle Bosché in The Purpose Factor *demonstrate that if you have a purpose anything is obtainable. So find your purpose."*

—**Marie Forleo**, *NYT* Bestselling Author of *Everything Is Figureoutable*

"Regardless of whatever I do, I know what my purpose is: to make a difference in people's lives. That is my purpose. What is yours? You need more than to just know what your purpose is, you need to understand how to carry out God's purpose for you. That is where The Purpose Factor *comes in. Brian and Gabrielle Bosché in this book not only help you discover your purpose but provide the plan to live your purpose as He wants you to."*

—**Tim Tebow**, Winner of the Heisman Trophy

"Mentally, every day I get my mind and body in the right place because I have a purpose. My purpose drives and motivates me. Find how to open up your purpose by reading The Purpose Factor. *Once you find your purpose, it will change your life."*

—**Simone Biles**, Five-Time Olympic Medalist

"Living passionately on-purpose and committed to your purpose makes life thrillingly worthwhile, enjoyable, and meaningful. This book will get your purposefulness to become a white-hot desire that has you rise higher and higher."

—**Mark Victor Hansen**, Founder & Co-Creator of the *Chicken Soup for the Soul* Series

"What you need more than anything else for success is a purpose. Find that purpose and succeed. The Purpose Factor *will unlock the way to find your life's purpose."*

—**Blake Mycoskie**, Founder and Chief Shoe Giver of TOMS Shoes

"You're crazy if you don't buy HUNDREDS of copies for your team—and make it required reading for your leaders! Your team's depth of purpose is directly connected to revenue and customer satisfaction."

—**Tamara Lowe**, *NYT* Bestselling Author of *Get Motivated!*

"If you want to find your purpose, you need to read this book. The Purpose Factor *is the clearest, most action-ready process to discover and use your purpose. Brian and Gabrielle are the next generation of motivators helping people achieve greatness."*

—**Tom Ziglar**, CEO, Ziglar Inc.

"One of Napoleon Hill's most important principles was having a major definite purpose, and great leaders know their purpose. Brian and Gabrielle bring new clarity, strategy, and insight to the subject of purpose."

—**Don Green**, President and Chairman of The Napoleon Hill Foundation

"Without a purpose, success cannot be achieved. Every great venture begins with a purpose. Discover your purpose and achieve success. The Purpose Factor *is the book you need for both."*

—**Gary Kelly**, CEO of Southwest Airlines

"This is an amazing book that will change your life forever. It shows you how to become absolutely clear about who you are, what you really want, and how to achieve all your goals."

—**Brian Tracy**, Motivational Legend

the purpose factor

Extreme Clarity for Why You're Here and What to Do About It

brian bosché

gabrielle bosché

Download Your Free Purpose Factor Journal:

PurposeFactorBook.com/journal

Contents

PART THREE

PART FOUR

1

Your Purpose Factor

You cannot un-know what you're about to discover.

In September 2017, a popular Japanese television program followed the lives of seven elderly people in the small city of Kyōtango. The ninety- to one-hundred-year-olds were filmed as they went about their day. They woke up, ate small meals, visited family, ran errands, and prepared for bed. It wasn't the kind of thrilling reality show content you would expect. So why produce it?

Kyōtango and the region around it have three times more residents over the age of one hundred than the rest of Japan. It has produced Olympic athletes, rock stars, and one of the oldest men in history. The producers of the Japanese show wanted to know what made Kyōtango so unique.

What they found was truly amazing.

Yes, the individuals they followed exercised daily and ate healthily. But they looked different on the inside—at least under a microscope. All seven of these Japanese men and women had unusually high levels of DHEA in their bloodstream. DHEA, considered the "longevity hormone," is linked to longer lifespans, lower cancer risk, and better memory.

So was it their diet or environment that caused their bodies to make more of this miracle hormone? Not necessarily. Every person in this region has an *ikigai*. Ikigai translates to "a reason for being" or "one's reason for waking up in the morning."

For these Japanese people, their ikigai is their purpose in life.

Whether the television producers realized it or not, they discovered an absolute truth. Purpose is the factor that makes life worth living. It doesn't simply add years to your life; it adds life to your years.

Purpose is the factor that makes the difference. It's the difference between simply existing and really living. Purpose simplifies decision-making. It makes better leaders, stronger companies, and happier people. Purpose determines the work you do, the relationships you have, and the life you live.

The pursuit of purpose is the pursuit to matter. And isn't that what we all want—to matter? Yet purpose is rarely a topic of conversation. We don't teach it in our schools or talk about it in houses of worship. We think it's irrelevant—or worse, inappropriate—to discuss at work.

Don't believe us? Bring up purpose at your next dinner party and get ready for blank stares. It's one of those topics like Blockchain or the Electoral College. We think we know what it is, but we'd have a hard time defining it if someone asked.

The word purpose has become meaningless. The discussion around purpose has become so broad, emotional, and ridiculous that it leaves one to think it can only be discovered at the top of a mountain or while gazing into a sunset.

Why We Were Wrong

That's what we believed. We thought finding our purpose was something that just happened. If you were lucky, you found it early. If you weren't so lucky, you had to wander through life waiting for someone else to show you your purpose and wondering if this is all there is.

We didn't discover our purpose until we were forced to. Before we met, each of us was having a crisis of purpose. Brian lost a marriage and his job in the same month. Gabrielle checked off all of the "supposed-to" boxes—degrees, jobs, income—but achievement wasn't enough. For all of the work we had done to plan our lives, our plans weren't working out. In a few short years, we had gone from brimming with potential to experiencing feelings of regret.

Both of us were asking life's biggest two-part question: **Why am I here and what am I supposed to do about it?**

We knew we needed help. Brian moved to Florida to be mentored by a motivational titan. Gabrielle sought mentorship from a top businesswoman in New York. Both mentors asked about our regrets, our mistakes, and our goals. They helped us admit what was obvious to everyone else: we weren't happy with how our lives were turning out.

After months of working with Brian, his mentor gave him simple advice: "You need to find your purpose." It was so simple that it felt like a throwaway line. Of course he should find his purpose, but he had no idea where to start.

At the time, Brian was selling self-help products from a one-bedroom apartment in South Florida. He was making just enough money to buy the six-dollar spaghetti sauce, but not enough to fix the broken glove box that hung open in his 2003 Volkswagen Jetta.

One afternoon, Brian was on a sales call that was going nowhere. He was speaking to a woman in her early fifties. Finally, out of frustration, she said, "I can't buy anything from you. I don't even know my purpose!" Here they were, on opposite sides of a sales call, both desperately searching for purpose and unable to make a decision about what to do next.

Over the next few weeks, Brian saw the "purpose problem" everywhere. It was why CEOs didn't lead their companies with authenticity. It was why students couldn't make decisions about their career path. It was why folks quit when they didn't get the promotion. It was why so many of us start projects and hobbies that never work out. Though he noticed the problem, he needed an answer.

So one day, Brian pulled out a legal pad and started writing down everything he had ever heard about purpose—what experts said, what ancient truths revealed, and what common sense suggested. By the time he was done, everything pointed to one truth. Purpose had just four elements, no sunset required. Those four elements were the secret to finding purpose and experiencing fulfillment. Finally, purpose didn't have to be a mystery. It wasn't only for the lucky few. The discovery of purpose was a process, and it was a process that could be followed by anyone.

After his breakthrough, Brian went back to doing sales calls for six to eight hours per day. Using his discovery, he went from selling products to helping people find their purpose. As a result, something miraculous happened. His sales numbers went up. His team grew. He was experiencing more fulfillment—and making more money, too.

Brian had found his purpose: to help others discover and live out their purpose by designing the most practical purpose-discovery process ever.

Who Not Why

All of us have or will experience a crisis of meaning in our lives. We experience them in the small moments while falling asleep at night. We experience them in the big moments when we lose a loved one or the stability of a job.

If you feel like we did before finding our purpose, you may feel like your life doesn't have clarity. You're not sure what's next. You're moving in a direction, but it doesn't feel intentional. It feels like life is happening to you, not because of you.

You distract yourself by checking email or planning vacations. You become addicted to checking off to-do lists and setting goals—even if they aren't the right goals—because planning feels like progress. But something doesn't feel right. There has to be more to life than running errands, getting paid, and meeting deadlines set by other people.

You wonder what could have been when a childhood friend launches a wildly successful podcast and lives your dream life. You question why your colleague gets the promotion over you or how your college roommate retired a multi-millionaire at age forty-five. You doubt your path when you see a product for sale that was your idea a decade ago. You go from happy to disappointed in a matter of moments. It's clear. You don't know your purpose.

On our path to discovering purpose, we found ourselves frustrated. We were told it's what makes you happy, it's providing for your family, or it's about finding your "why." We were taught purpose is a feeling, not an action. Or worse, that purpose is the same thing as passion. Everything we heard about purpose led to a dead end. It all sounded good, but it wasn't good.

When we made our purpose about "why," we created short-term motivation, not long-term clarity. Your "why" will change. It will shift. It will adjust to the season you are in and the work you are doing. "Why" could be getting your kids through school or finding a husband. It could be taking care of your aging parents or losing weight to make your ex jealous. All are strong motivators, but they're not your purpose. Simply put, if you want to know how to be motivated, ask *Why*? If you want to find purpose, ask *Who*?

In a basic sense, purpose is the reason something or someone exists. Your phone charger has a purpose. Your raincoat has a purpose. Your bank account has a purpose. Each was designed to serve a purpose by solving a problem for *someone*. Purpose is always about "who."

When Sara Blakely invented Spanx, she started with "who," not "why." Her "who" was herself. She couldn't find shapewear that worked, so she designed her own and solved the same problem for millions of other women. The viral "ALS Ice Bucket Challenge" raised over 200 million dollars in three years because of who it impacted. The disease was not widely known until the story of Pete Frates—who suffered from and eventually died from the disease—went viral. When Fred Rogers launched his public television show, *Mister Rogers' Neighborhood*, his "who" were young children. When you look behind every great leader, invention, and movement, it was started by people that knew who they were and who they were supposed to help.

What we thought about purpose wasn't working for one reason: we were making it about us, not others. Traditional definitions of purpose make it about us. Our passions. Our priorities. Our preferences. When we make purpose about us and our happiness, we come up short. When we make purpose about others and what we can do for them, we experience fulfillment.

Discovering and living out your purpose is about answering this two-part question: **Who am I, and who am I supposed to help?**

Answer in the wrong order, and you'll miss your purpose altogether. Answer in the right order, and you will live with the kind of fulfillment and meaning you have been craving.

Purpose Is the Factor

When Brian discovered the four elements of finding purpose, he noticed something: these four elements, when understood and applied in the right order, made one major difference. They became a factor that changed everything. Brian had come to realize that every conversation he had about purpose was wrong. We shouldn't look at purpose as the reason we exist. Purpose is the factor that defines who we are and who we are supposed to help.

Simply put, your purpose is what you have to help others.

Purpose is the factor that makes the difference. If you want to make a difference, you must discover your Purpose Factor.

When you know your Purpose Factor, you focus on what you have, not what you don't have. You stop comparing yourself to others and shut down self-doubt. You realize that you're here for a reason. That reason is to help others with what's inside of you. You're more confident, more competent, and more productive. You recognize that you can connect what you do every day to the impact that you want to have. And, you discover that living a life of fulfillment doesn't happen by accident. It requires a process.

The Purpose Factor gives you a simple process to discover and live out your purpose. It has been taught to the United States military and stay-at-home moms. It is used by local sales representatives and international nonprofits. It works whether you are a student or retiree, if you are married or single, or if you are a new hire or well established in your career.

We wrote this book for people like you who know there's more to life than going through the motions. Discovering your Purpose Factor is the first step, but not the most important step. Your action is the secret to making this work.

In this book, you will discover exactly what you have to help others and how to use your Purpose Factor to achieve your goals. You will learn how to experience real, maximum fulfillment in every area of your life. You will gain more clarity than ever before on where you're going and how you'll get there. More than that, you'll adopt a mindset that will change the way you live each day.

When you discover your Purpose Factor, everything changes. Every day matters. Every setback has significance. Money comes easier. Relationships prosper. You do more than get by; you are pulled by what you have to help others.

You've lived long enough without the clarity you crave. It's time to go from simply existing to really living.

2

Figuring Out What's Next

Have you ever looked at the lives of the most fulfilled and wondered, "What do they know that I don't?" You think: "Why do they make more of an impact? Why do they have more influence, make more money, and have more joy? Why does their life seem to make more sense?" Some people believe that money or your station in life determine the answers to those questions. But why is it that so many high-impact people came from nothing?

The answer: the Purpose Factor was at work.

Your Purpose Factor is what you have to help others. **Fulfillment is the result of helping others with what you have.** To experience maximum fulfillment, the goal is simple. You must align every part of your life to your purpose. If you don't, you'll feel the effects. It's like going through life with a misaligned spine or a piece of gravel stuck in your shoe. You can make it through, but it's agonizing.

Alignment with your purpose is the goal. That's because alignment produces clarity, motivation, and results. Yes, even financial results. And to align your life with your purpose requires a process. Having the right process is critical to your success. In life, you can have the right goals but the wrong process and never achieve those goals. However, if you have the right goals and the right process, you're unstoppable.

Successful people know this. They know that every breakthrough in life is designed and achieved through a process. Saving money requires a process. Paying off debt requires a process.

Losing weight and keeping it off requires a process. Having a stable marriage requires a process. Raising well-behaved kids requires a process. Every achievement requires a process, yet we leave finding our purpose to chance.

For a long time, purpose has lacked a process for both discovery and application. You were more likely to find your purpose by luck or fate, until now.

Introducing the Elements of the Purpose Factor

The Purpose Factor is the proven four-step process that we discovered and developed through years of testing and scores of iterations. It has been built, broken down, reorganized, turned upside down, and put back together. It reveals the steps you must take to discover your purpose and get extreme clarity on what to do with it.

The Purpose Factor is made up of four elements. We will briefly define those elements and show how each of them flow together to power the Purpose Factor. In later chapters, we will lead you through a series of questions to help you understand the four elements of your Purpose Factor, and show you how to use them to get incredible results. These elements are arranged in a specific order of discovery—designed to take you by the hand and guide you step by step:

1. Natural Advantage—The role you tend to play.
2. Acquired Skills—The abilities you acquired and developed.
3. Pull-Passion—The problem you're made to solve.
4. Origin Story—The moment that most shaped your perspective.

You see the elements of the Purpose Factor in the lives of entrepreneurs, history-makers, top athletes, and the happiest people you know. Once you understand how the elements work, you'll see how their Natural Advantage showed these individuals where to start, their Acquired Skills increased their value, their Pull-Passion motivated them to succeed, and their Origin Story gave them a reason to help others.

Whether they knew it or not, the Purpose Factor was shaping their identity, increasing their influence, broadening their impact, and building their income.

The Identity Factor

> *When you know your purpose, you know who you are and who you can help.*

People living out their Purpose Factor have extreme clarity as to who they are, what they have, and how to use it to help others. No matter their setbacks or bad breaks, their purpose becomes synonymous with who they are.

When you take time to find your Purpose Factor, you get extreme clarity on who you are, who you can help, and why you matter. When no one else believes in you, you'll keep going because you know who you're here to help. You no longer crave their approval because you're pulled by something bigger.

> *"I believe all of us are here on planet earth to learn how to give what we have been given. That's your job—to figure out how you're going to be used for a purpose greater than yourself."*
> ***—Oprah Winfrey***

Oprah Winfrey's Purpose Factor redefined the role of women in media. As a child, her Natural Advantage was obvious. She was a natural communicator. She would ask questions of her dolls and the crows on the fence. Oprah started to cultivate her Acquired Skills in journalism while in high school. By the time she was nineteen years old, she had a job in radio. After college, she held multiple positions in local television before taking a Chicago morning talk show to national syndication.

An observation of Oprah's life would reveal a Pull-Passion for helping others overcome adversity. Her overcomer Origin Story is compelling. The daughter of a teenage mother, she was sexually molested multiple times and, at age fourteen, became pregnant. Her son was born prematurely and died shortly after birth. Despite setbacks and struggles in her early career, that Chicago talk show became the *Oprah Winfrey Show*. After its debut in 1986, it was the highest-rated national talk show for twenty-four consecutive seasons. Oprah's brand is the delivery vehicle for her Purpose Factor, which she has used to inspire millions.

Like Oprah, Dwayne "The Rock" Johnson used his Purpose Factor to escape obscurity and be seen for who he was. Dwayne was a natural athlete, but he was also naturally empathetic and protective. He has been able to use that Natural Advantage of caring for others to develop a career and a brand full of personality.

Sometimes Acquired Skills are by choice. Sometimes they are forced upon you. Dwayne had to develop skills in personal branding as he struggled to find his identity in wrestling. He went through four different stage names and was booed by twenty thousand fans his first time in the ring. Reflecting on that moment, Dwayne said, "It wasn't me personally that they didn't like. It was that I wasn't being me." Dwayne learned quickly and found his Pull-Passion for entertaining others at the start of his wrestling career.

Dwayne's Origin Story was formed over many years of rejection and setback. Before he was sixteen, Dwayne and his family were evicted, their car was repossessed, and he was arrested eight times. He tried to pursue a professional NFL career but was never drafted. He was kicked off a Canadian football team. He was on the brink of homelessness just before his wrestling career took off. But through it all, Dwayne prevailed. He went from having seven dollars in his pocket to becoming the highest-paid actor in the world and named among the "100 Most Influential People" by *Time* magazine.

The Influence Factor

When you know your purpose, you become an influencer.

Your Purpose Factor unlocks positive change in the lives of those around you. When we use our purpose to help others, we earn trust, respect, and influence. Powerful things happen when we understand that our purpose is not about us. It's about what's inside of us to help others—and using influence to make it happen.

Sheryl Sandberg used her Purpose Factor to define her influence and inspire women to stop doubting their power. Sheryl knew how to study. She was a self-starter and hardworking student. Her Natural Advantage informed her choice to study economics. She graduated summa cum laude from Harvard and went on to develop skills in monetizing web search at Google.

But it was in college that Sheryl discovered her Pull-Passion. She noticed few women joining her Harvard classes and co-founded the student organization Women in Economics and Government. The thread of advocacy is woven through her Origin Story. Sheryl's parents helped Jews escaping anti-Semitism from the former Soviet Union. But Sheryl's defining moment came while hearing a speech on imposter syndrome as a student. It helped her realize how she, and women like her, did not fully believe in their potential. Sheryl is now the chief operating officer of Facebook. She is the bestselling author of multiple books and has helped women worldwide recognize what they have to offer.

It's hard to define where influence ends and leadership begins. That's because leadership is influence. The more people follow you, the more influence you have. The more influence you have, the more that people will trust what you say. Tennis legend Billie Jean King is the ultimate example of that.

> *"Natural talent only determines the limits of your athletic potential. It's dedication and a willingness to discipline your life that makes you great."* —**Billie Jean King**

Billie Jean King used her Purpose Factor to demand equality for women in sports. Billie Jean was naturally athletic, but she found tennis when a childhood friend invited her to a local country club. Her parents couldn't afford expensive country club lessons or equipment. Billie Jean's father told her to "figure it out." She did. Billie Jean did odd jobs for neighbors and eventually saved $9.28 to buy her first tennis racquet. She even took free lessons at public courts. Billie was determined to build the skills to become the best tennis player in the world.

At age twelve, she started to notice something. Tennis was for a select few who wore white, were white, and weren't women. Out of that Origin Story, she found her Pull-Passion. She would dedicate her life to fighting for equal rights. But to do that, she needed a platform. Title after title, Billie Jean became the best. At the height of her career in 1973, she successfully lobbied the U.S. Open to award equal prize money for men and women. That same year, she co-founded the Women's Tennis Association. She defeated Bobby Riggs—a self-proclaimed chauvinist—in the famous Battle of the Sexes.

Influence is not given. It must be earned. For those who tap into their Purpose Factor, influence flows faster and spreads wider, creating heroes and starting movements.

The Impact Factor

> *When you know your purpose, you can change the world around you.*

When you leverage all four elements of the Purpose Factor to help people, your impact is guaranteed. To help others, you must use your purpose to do one of three things: solve problems, satisfy needs, or heal brokenness. Do that, and it's impossible not to change the world. It isn't the process of discovering your purpose that makes an impact. It's living out your purpose that changes everyone and everything for the better.

> *"Action without vision is only passing time, vision without action is merely daydreaming, but vision with action can change the world."* —***Nelson Mandela***

You may know the name Nelson Mandela. You may not know that his global impact was shaped in a small village in South Africa. Nelson had a Natural Advantage for organizing others and was given the indigenous name for "troublemaker" as a child. The first in his family to get an education, Nelson sharpened his skills by going to law school. He served as a lawyer in

Johannesburg before publicly speaking out against apartheid, the government-instituted racial discrimination in South Africa.

Nelson was passionate about justice and equality. His Origin Story began with him being the son of a well-respected local chief who died when Nelson was young; his father's life and death inspired him to defend not only his people but anyone considered a second-class citizen. Though his Pull-Passion landed him in prison for twenty-seven years, he became the first democratically elected president of South Africa. Nelson used his Purpose Factor to bring about racial reconciliation in South Africa and spark a global civil rights movement.

Entrepreneur Titan Gilroy used his Purpose Factor to transform an industry. Titan was a natural builder and artist. Math and art were the only school subjects he was good at; the rest he failed. A small kid growing up in a bad neighborhood, Titan developed skills in boxing to protect himself from bullies. A long line of undefeated street fights got him noticed by the likes of Dick Sadler, who trained both Muhammad Ali and George Foreman. Though he had a promising career ahead of him, a bar fight landed him a sixteen-year prison sentence. After his release from prison, he put violence behind him and went to work in manufacturing. He leveraged what he acquired from boxing speed drills to increase his work station's output.

His story gave him a Pull-Passion for giving people second chances, especially those in prison. He now owns a manufacturing company and offers free online training to those who want to learn his craft. Titan even built a machine shop inside San Quentin State Prison to give inmates a skill and apply their purpose after their release. His talents, skills, Pull-Passion, and story all align to transform the lives of others.

Take a close look at any successful person, and you will notice that the elements of the Purpose Factor are in alignment. When the elements work together, they show you what to do and how to do it. Every person who has made an impact did so with their Purpose Factor.

The Income Factor

> *When you know your purpose, you can use it to make a difference and more money.*

The point of life is not to make money. However, wealth becomes a platform for our purpose when we use it to help others. The truly fulfilled have learned how to use their Purpose Factor to build a life and make a living. They use their Purpose Factor to determine how they spend their time, invest their money, and focus their attention.

Sir Richard Branson turned his Purpose Factor into an empire that serves millions of customers worldwide. As a kid with dyslexia, he was a natural overcomer and go-getter. Richard was also a risk-taker. He started his first company at sixteen years old after dropping out of school. Ironically, it was a magazine called *Student.* He sold $8,000 in advertisements for the first edition. That funded his next venture, Virgin Records.

Through the beginning of his entrepreneurial journey, Richard developed his Acquired Skills in business growth. He would always run one company to fund the start of another. It wasn't just business that he loved. Richard was passionate about helping people. As a teen, he started his first charity to help other young people overcome setback.

His Origin Story? Right before Richard dropped out of school, his headmaster told him, "You will either go to prison or become a millionaire." He chose the latter and became one of the most recognized billionaires in the world, famous for his investments and unconventional personality.

Amazon founder and CEO Jeff Bezos leveraged his Purpose Factor to revolutionize the way we live our lives and buy our products. Experimentation and solving problems came naturally to him. As a kid, Jeff spent his summers fixing things on his grandparents' ranch in Texas. His makeshift alarm systems would keep his younger siblings out of his room. Jeff developed skillsets in engineering and computer science at Princeton University. Once he started working, Jeff quickly honed his skills in business—becoming the youngest senior vice president at a Wall Street investment firm.

As for his Pull-Passion, take a close look, and you'll see that Jeff is passionate about increasing access. His company Amazon provides customers with increased access to millions of products. His space company, Blue Origin, seeks to create access to more energy solutions as demand for resources increases. Even in high school, he started a club to give students access to their creative-thinking peers. His Origin Story is powerful. His mother was just seventeen years old when Jeff was born. Growing up, Jeff did not have a relationship with his biological father. His stepfather, Miguel Bezos, is a Cuban refugee. Miguel emigrated to the United States as a teenager after his parents lost their factory to the Cuban government. Now one of the wealthiest men in the world, Jeff Bezos's Purpose Factor has changed the lives of millions by increasing access to the world's products.

Now that the curtain is pulled back on how the Purpose Factor works and who it works for, can you see the elements start to come together? The application is endless. The secret of the Purpose Factor is at work in the lives of all successful people. It's centuries of wisdom distilled in a simple four-step formula.

The world has taught us that people like Billie Jean King, Oprah Winfrey, and Jeff Bezos were lucky, but that would devalue their story and yours. Explaining away the proof of the Purpose Factor is dangerous. "They were lucky," "Things just worked for them," and "Right idea, right timing kinda thing" are all throwaway phrases that trick us into believing that purpose is something to be caught rather than something to be pursued. But it isn't. Your purpose is too important to be left to chance. It's time to see the Purpose Factor in action.

Aligning the elements of your Purpose Factor is the key to living a life of meaning. It's worked for us and, if you let it, it will work for you.

3

The Pursuit to Matter

Brian had just landed in Colorado for an event. He had been up since 4:00 a.m. and was looking forward to a hot shower and a quick nap at the hotel before afternoon meetings. He grabbed his bag from baggage claim, called an Uber, and waited for a Toyota Corolla driven by Andrew.

Minutes later, Andrew arrived and Brian jumped in the back seat. After exchanging hellos and friendly banter, Andrew asked Brian a series of questions. What was he doing in Colorado? How long was he here? What did he do for a living?

As they drove through the bright Colorado morning, Brian shared that he speaks and writes—and that he was working on a new book. The subject? Purpose.

Andrew responded, "Really? I need to know my purpose."

Brian said, "Tell me more about that."

Brian was secretly waiting for Andrew to say he was a thirty-five-year-old billionaire and only did this for fun on the weekends. Or maybe he was working as an undercover reporter doing a story on Uber passenger behavior. But he wasn't. Andrew had a story we've heard before.

Prior to driving for Uber, Andrew worked in video production—and he was good at it. During the twenty-minute ride, Andrew talked about how much he liked video production but hated the politics of working in an office. He spoke about how he once raised over sixty thousand dollars for a Kickstarter project. Andrew talked, and Brian listened. Andrew said things like, "I'm in transition," and "I'm figuring out what's next."

This would have been understandable if his transition had been a few weeks or months. But it had been seven years.

Brian knew what was really going on. Behind the responsible-sounding explanation was the real story. Truth be told, Andrew was stuck, and he didn't know what to do.

Perhaps you feel like Andrew. From the outside, it looks like you've got it all together. On the inside, you're treading water, waiting for life to make sense around you. Maybe you feel stuck because you got burned in the past. Maybe a temporary setback made you feel like a lifetime failure. Maybe you feel too old for the dream that you had when you were younger. Or maybe you did what you were supposed to do. You went to school and got a job. Then you figured out it wasn't what you wanted after all.

When you were young, you felt unstoppable. Now you can't seem to get started. You may be stuck, but you don't have to stay there. There's a Chinese proverb that adequately depicts the nature of unrealized dreams, which says, "The best time to plant a tree was twenty years ago. The second-best time is now." The only difference between yesterday's dreams and today's reality is the passage of time. Those dreams that you had of greatness, of success, of impacting others are still possible. In fact, with all of the growth in your talents, skills, and life experience, those dreams may be more possible.

What Andrew told Brian was something we hear often. "I need to figure out what's next," "I'm looking for more direction in my life," or "I'm waiting to get more clarity." The phrases are different, but they mean the same thing: I don't know what to do.

The people who need purpose the most put off finding it the longest. They feel there's no time to consider finding their purpose. That's because when times are tough, money is tight, and tensions are high, you think purpose will have to wait.

But it can't wait. Here's the real truth: the key to figuring out right now and figuring out what's next is to discover your Purpose Factor.

Knowing your purpose is critical to getting your next move right. If you don't know your purpose, your next move won't have context. If you don't know your purpose, you may choose to do something that feels right, but isn't right for you. Oftentimes, we jump from experience to experience or job to job because it feels like progress, but in reality, we're living the same day over and over. Then you're back at square one, trying to figure out what's next...again.

Before you figure out right now and what's next, you have to answer two questions. First, "How did I get here?" And second, "What will keep me from moving forward?"

How Did I Get Here?

It's not often that the two of us see a movie in theaters. If we do watch a movie, it may be months or years after its initial release. That was the case when we sat down to watch *The Wedding Date*. (Brian wanted to clarify that Gabrielle made him watch *The Wedding Date*, which he liked.)

It's a 2005 romantic comedy starring Debra Messing and Dermot Mulroney. The plot of the movie is simple. Debra's character, Kat, needs a date for her sister's wedding and ends up hiring an escort named Nick, Dermot's character, to go with her. At one point during the movie, Kat is complaining about her love life to Nick.

Nick responds, "Every woman has the exact love life she wants."

There it was, a diamond of a principle hidden in the predictable storyline of a rom-com. We all have the kinds of jobs, waistlines, and love lives that we want. Why? Because if we wanted something different, we would have acted to change it. We act on what we believe.

Where we are today represents all the decisions that we did or didn't make, whether they were proactive decisions about our direction or reactive decisions in response to circumstances. Where we are is where we are. What we've achieved is what we've achieved. What we've got is what we've got. We chose it.

The secret to figuring out what's next is recognizing where you're at, and that requires ownership. Eleanor Roosevelt wrote:

> *One's philosophy is not best expressed in words; it is expressed in the choices one makes. In the long run, we shape our lives, and we shape ourselves. The process never ends until we die. And the choices we make are ultimately our own responsibility.*

Ownership allows you to acknowledge the past and create the future. It helps you discover your Purpose Factor and define what's next.

Many of us avoid pursuing purpose because we don't want to be disappointed. What if we can't achieve it? What if it's too late? What if we missed our chance?

We would venture to say most people suffer from extreme disappointment. Disappointed in a relationship because it didn't last. Disappointed in a job because it didn't work out. Disappointed by family members because they let you down. Disappointed in themselves because they should have it figured out by now.

All disappointment comes down to unmet expectations.

So let's consider these questions: What did you expect your life to include by now? More money? Better relationships? More influence? True fulfillment?

Expectations shape how you react to the world, but purpose shapes how you see the world.

There are only two explanations for why you are disappointed: either you are not achieving your expectations because they are unrealistic, or they are realistic, but your reality is not aligned with your expectations. The only way to escape disappointment is to discover and use your Purpose Factor.

What Will Keep Me From Moving Forward?

We have noticed two things while helping people get clarity about their Purpose Factor. First, folks who don't know their purpose jump from experience to experience without direction. And second, people confuse their desire to change and their potential to improve with the action required to make it happen.

When it came to Andrew's future, it wasn't that he lacked the desire or potential to be successful. During the drive, he was incredibly hopeful. He believed that a better future was possible. Lack of desire or potential likely isn't your problem either. It's a lack of action.

You want to know your purpose. Despite your setbacks and frustration, you expect the future to be different—to be better. Desire is important. You have to want to change before anything will improve. But desire alone is not enough. Cemeteries are full of dreams that died at the stage of desire.

There's nothing wrong with having potential. Potential is powerful. But we confuse potential with progress. We think that at any time we can change, and maybe that's even more dangerous. We tell ourselves we can find another job when we're ready, leave the relationship at any point, go back to school when things slow down, or start writing the book next week. This works for a while. It gives us a sense of control without requiring action. We become fixated with our potential to change and our plans to improve, but we never take action.

We were curious about the definition of "potential," so we looked it up. Potential is defined as "latent abilities that may be developed and lead to future success." Notice the word "latent," which means hidden or not yet developed. That's the problem with potential. We are capable of great things, but until potential turns into practice, our impact is invisible.

Think about this in terms of energy. Energy is all around us. It's the hum of electricity powering our refrigerators and iPhones. It's a car driving down the street. But there are two types of energy: potential energy and kinetic energy. Potential energy is what an object could do if the right forces acted upon it. Kinetic energy is the energy of an object once in motion. Your parked car is full of potential energy, but it will remain hidden in your garage until you take action to put it in motion.

How do you do that? You take your hand, start the car, put it in gear, and place your foot on the accelerator. Your key cranks the starter, which fires the spark plugs, which ignite the proper mixture of gasoline and air, and the car goes forward. Potential becomes kinetic. Your Purpose Factor is the car in the garage. It is only useful when you take action to put it in motion.

The greatest writers, leaders, entrepreneurs, and parents move beyond potential. When your Purpose Factor is what you have to help others, then everything you have is a gift to help others. Every talent is a gift. Every skill is a gift. Every setback is a gift.

No matter what you've achieved or what you've been through, you can use it to help others. All of it is a gift, so own it. Ownership is freedom. When you own it all, you stop blaming others for where you are. Ownership allows you to acknowledge the past and create the future. It helps you discover your Purpose Factor and define what's next.

This book will give you clarity on today, tomorrow, and how to shape your future. If you only focus on the present, you will remain stuck. If all you do is focus on the future, you will never get there. Your Purpose Factor is the bridge between the two.

The key to figuring out what's next is to address what you believe about purpose. Before we can guide you through your Purpose Factor, we must break down some of the lies and half-truths that keep us from living fulfilled lives. With the purpose barriers removed, we will show you how to get extreme clarity in life and work.

Who am I, and who am I supposed to help?

Part One

The Myths: What We Thought Purpose Was

Introduction

For years, we had the wrong definition of purpose.

We thought purpose was all about achievement. Everything was about our success—what we wore, who we knew, and what we did on the weekend. The truth was we were broke, insecure, and grasping for a clear direction. This made us doubt who we were and what we had to offer. We tried tapping into passion, but passion was fleeting—there one day and gone the next. We wanted to know our purpose. We wanted to know what was next, but were looking in all of the wrong places.

Most people have the wrong definition of purpose. We certainly did. Those wrong definitions distract us from finding our true purpose and using it to help others. They cause us to look for purpose in relationships, achievements, hobbies, and happiness. Here is what we found. If you follow the wrong definition of purpose, you will experience what we experienced: heartbreak, frustration, and anxiety about your own worth.

We hit rock bottom. A few times.

We know what it's like to wonder if your car is going to get repossessed. Whenever we heard the trash truck, we thought our car was getting towed away. We know what it's like to have your water shut off while you're taking a shower because you didn't pay the bill, shampoo still in your hair. Or how it feels to let go of your entire team because you couldn't pay them.

We said everything was fine on the outside, but on the inside, we wondered if we would make it. We posted inspirational messages on social media about how happy we were while feeling anxious and depressed. We thought we needed to be more positive about the situation. We listened to inspirational gurus, watched pump-up videos, and read the self-help books. None of it worked.

Everything we read seemed to contradict the last thing we read. We needed bigger goals. We needed smaller goals. We needed to track our tasks. We shouldn't track tasks. We should get faster computers. We needed to become minimalists. We needed to say yes. We needed to say no.

So what did we do?

We threw out what sounded good and focused on what was good. We got real about who we were and who we could help. We stopped focusing on *why* we were working and started focusing on *who* we were helping. We quickly realized that we were frustrated because we had made life all about us. **We found our purpose by asking, "Who am I, and who can I help?"** When we did, every sale, every hire, and every conversation went from being us-centered to others-centered.

We spent less time on social media. It was just a comparison trap anyway. We simplified our morning routines and dropped our addiction to motivational mantras. We took back our lives. We stopped trying to be motivated and became more motivated than ever.

Our journey proved what you believe about purpose will determine how quickly you discover it. In this next section, we reveal the biggest myths about purpose. Those myths confuse purpose with goals, passion, duty, and happiness. Each myth, if believed, will stop you from discovering your Purpose Factor. Before finding and using your Purpose Factor, we will destroy what's holding you back.

4

Setting Big Goals

Are your goals your purpose?

Every year, 45 percent of Americans make New Year's resolutions, while only 8 percent actually follow through. That's 147 million people setting goals each January and 135 million giving up. Gyms are joined, planners are purchased, and promises are made to be better next year. But then life happens, priorities change, and we don't get around to achieving much.

So why make resolutions in the first place?

A 2015 study focused on why people make and then ignore their New Year's resolutions. The study found that the top three reasons people admitted they gave up on their goals were:

- Their goals were unrealistic,
- They didn't measure their progress, or
- They forgot about their goals altogether.

In other words, they gave up on their goals because they failed to turn their plans into their priorities. We see top-performing athletes giving advice about having big goals. We hear business titans telling us the secret to success is bigger goals. We read in self-help books that bigger goals and better goals are the only way to make it to the top. So does having goals make life more meaningful?

In 1953, the Yale University graduating class was asked, "How many of you have specific, written down goals?" The answer: 3 percent. Twenty years later, researchers went back to check in on the class of 1953. Here was their discovery: the 3 percent who had written their goals down had made more money than the other 97 percent combined.

The lessons of this study could not be more clear: people with goals succeed. People without goals fail.

The only problem? The study never happened.

The now-famous study has been used in motivational speeches, self-help books, and pep talks for years. However, there is no proof that the study exists. Researchers from Harvard University, Dominican University, and Fast Company's investigative unit all went looking for the legendary study and came up short.

The Yale goal-setting study was believed to be true because we all wanted it to be true. We want to believe that simply setting goals and sticking to them will guarantee success. We've come to think that our goals (or lack of them) are holding us back from more money, losing weight, finding a partner, or finally retiring. But goals aren't the problem. The problem is a lack of purpose.

Glamorized Stuck-ness

The world has glamorized, even systematized, goal setting. Google "goal tracking" and you'll get over 352 million search results. There are planners designed and peddled to all types of niches—moms, students, entrepreneurs, and executives.

Don't want to write your goals in a normal planner? There are special pens that write on special paper that magically uploads to the cloud. These apps and gadgets make us feel like we're closer to our dreams. But in reality, we're no closer to achieving them.

We've also glamorized goal setting's little sisters: to-do lists. These are the lists that help us achieve our goals. On these lists, we jot down housework, homework, holiday shopping, and anything else we don't want to forget. Just writing a list down feels productive, doesn't it? But being productive is not the same as being purposeful. **You can live an entire life of achievement and completely miss your purpose.**

We fell for it too. We got the fitness trackers, downloaded the checklist apps, and read the books about growing your goals. When one goal was too hard or too complicated, we replaced it with another, more achievable one. When we had checked everything off of one list, we immediately started creating another one—never questioning if these were the right tasks or the right goals.

Big thinking, goal tracking, and to-do lists are not inherently bad. Like any tool, it depends on how you use it.

Right Ladder, Wrong Wall

If purpose is what you have to help others, and fulfillment is the result of helping others with what you have, then what are goals? Goals are aims or desired results. Without knowing your purpose, you risk "aiming" in the wrong direction. We've been idolizing goals, and ignoring what makes our goals matter.

The late Stephen Covey draws a big red circle around this point. He suggested that many people like to rush up the ladder of life, but as he said, "If the ladder is not leaning against the right wall, every step we take just gets us to the wrong place faster."

In other words, you may be working towards something, but it may not be the right thing. Setting goals that are not aligned with your purpose is putting your ladder against the wrong wall. You'll get somewhere, but perhaps not where you want to be.

One of the biggest mistakes we make is believing that our goals are our purpose. They're not. **Our goals, if made correctly, keep us accountable on the path to living out our purpose.**

There are three types of goals—achievement, life events, and hygiene goals.

Achievement goals involve getting promoted to vice president of the company, running a marathon, or writing a book. Life event goals are major occasions such as going to college, getting a job, getting married, and having kids. Hygiene goals are actions like paying bills, paying off debt, staying healthy, and being a good husband or friend.

We confuse all three of these goals with our purpose. When we do, we make life about what we want to do, not who we want to help. And if you're not helping others, you're not experiencing true fulfillment.

Now there's nothing wrong with goals. Where we get off track is setting goals without asking: "Are my goals in alignment with my purpose? Are my achievement goals leveraging what's inside of me to help as many people as possible? Are my life event goals growing my ability to use my purpose? Are my hygiene goals helping me or distracting me from using my Purpose Factor to help others?"

Goals are not the enemy. Goals are only helpful when you align them with your Purpose Factor.

Go Beyond Goals

It had been twenty-one years since Dale sat in a restaurant. The sixty-five-year-old was released from prison that morning. Now he was sitting in a Denny's, overwhelmed by his breakfast options. Since he had been away for so long, he didn't know how to order food. Were there twelve types of egg dishes before he went in? Since when could you order breakfast all day?

Dale's goal had been to get out of prison, but no one had prepared him for life after prison. Experts say the first week is the most dangerous for newly released inmates. In fact, 83 percent will return to prison within nine years of getting out.

Dale didn't want to be another statistic, but he was unsure about what to do next. He had focused so much on the goal of getting out. Now, what was he supposed to do? Getting out was supposed to be the moment that gave him extreme clarity, but it didn't. That's because a goal is not your purpose. A goal is a step on the path to living out your purpose. Dale needed to discover his Purpose Factor.

Working with his reentry coaches, Dale was able to identify what he was good at (Natural Advantage), what his abilities were (Acquired Skills), what would motivate him (Pull-Passion), and what he had overcome (Origin Story). By discovering what he had to help others, he would be able to stay out of prison and experience true fulfillment.

Maybe you're like Dale. You have waited so long for something to happen—like getting married, getting promoted, or having a child. When that moment finally did happen, you didn't know what to do next. You got there, and you wondered why you didn't feel as fulfilled or happy as you thought you would. Or maybe you did experience extreme joy, but that joy faded as regular life started again.

That's because your goals are not your purpose. Making life about setting and achieving goals leads to a busy schedule and impressive resume, but it will not produce true fulfillment, impact, and meaning. When you discover your Purpose Factor, goals become mile markers on the road to using what you have to help others. They become moments of celebration and achievement. They help you measure how far you've come, but they are not the destination. When you know your Purpose Factor, goals are simply the steps to living it out.

5

Pursuing Passion

*"While passion is way too important to be without, it is way too fickle to follow around." —**Mike Rowe***

Is your passion your purpose?

The 2006 comedy *Talladega Nights* tells the story of Ricky Bobby, a NASCAR superstar who loses his wealth, wife, and fame and must fight to get it all back. The sports parody features comedian Will Ferrell as Ricky Bobby, working for the approval of his irresponsible, deadbeat dad, Reese Bobby, played by Gary Cole.

At the beginning of the movie, Reese tells his son, "Always remember, if you ain't first, you're last." This becomes the mantra of Ricky's life, taking him to the top of NASCAR. Years later, Ricky is reunited with his dad and confronts him about that advice.

Ricky: "I did just like you told me. If you ain't first, you're last."

Reese: "What the [heck] you talking about?"

Ricky: "What you told me that day at school for career day. You came in, and you said, 'If you ain't first, you're last.'"

Reese: "Ah [heck], Ricky, I was high when I said that. That doesn't make any sense at all. You could be second. You could be third. You could be fourth. [Heck], you could even be fifth."

Ricky: "What are you talking about? I lived my whole life based on that. Now, what the [heck] am I supposed to do?"

Reese: "Well, that's the million-dollar question, isn't it?"

Like Ricky, we all have beliefs that guide our lives, and those beliefs determine our actions. Our guiding beliefs come from many places: how we were raised, where we grew up, what we were taught, and what we've read. Some of those beliefs are good. Some beliefs are harmful, even illogical, and they hold us back from living our best life.

Society would have us believe that passion is the most important thing in life. But it isn't.

This belief causes us to think we should only work jobs that we love, or we can't marry someone unless we have a fairy-tale first date. In other words, if passion isn't there from the start, it isn't worth pursuing. And yet, when we pause and think, we realize how untrue this belief really is.

Every minute of your workday isn't going to bring you joy. Some of the best relationships have rocky starts. So while "Pursue your passion," feels like good advice to give and get, the results can be dangerous. That's because "your passion" may lead you in the wrong direction for months, years, and maybe even decades.

The Problem with Passion Alone

Today the word passion is misused and overused. It has so many meanings that it has no meaning at all. If you ask most people what passion means to them, they'll say, "It's something you really love doing," or, "It's something you get excited about," or worse, "It's something that makes you happy." More on happiness later.

As a result, we say we're passionate about coffee, but really, we enjoy coffee. That doesn't mean we should start a coffee shop. We say we're passionate about fitness, but really, we enjoy working out. That doesn't mean we should start a gym. We say we're passionate about golf, but really, it's just our favorite hobby. That doesn't mean we should be on the Pro Golf Tour. We are misusing the word passion to explain aspects of life we enjoy.

So what does the word "passion" mean? Passion is defined as a "barely controllable emotion." Interesting. If you were to replace the word "passion" with its dictionary definition in conversation, it would sound strange. "Follow your barely controllable emotions" would be terrible advice for a room of hormonal students. Graduation cards and speeches touting, "Don't do anything unless you have a barely controllable emotion for it," would sound less profound.

Let's make this more ridiculous. Below are some famous quotes by famous people about passion. The names are left out to protect the innocent.

- "Always go with your passions. Never ask yourself if it's realistic or not."
- "No alarm clock needed. My passion wakes me."
- "Dreams and passion are more powerful than facts and reality."
- "Turn your passion into your paycheck."

Each of these sound so good, but they transform into terrible advice when you replace the word passion with its dictionary definition.

- Always go with your barely controllable emotions. Never ask yourself if they're realistic or not.
- No alarm clock needed. My barely controllable emotion wakes me up.

- Dreams and barely controllable emotions are more powerful than facts and reality.
- Turn your barely controllable emotion into your paycheck.

These revised quotes won't end up on office inspirational posters or greeting cards any time soon. They sound stupid because they are stupid.

"Follow Your Passion" = Terrible Advice

In 2008, there were 34,642 graduates with history majors. But in 2017, just nine years later, the number of graduates with history majors fell to only 24,266. It left admission counselors scratching their heads. Were fewer students passionate about history in 2017 than in 2008? Did something happen over those nine years that caused students to be less interested in history? Perhaps, but it's more likely that the recession caused students to think more practically about their career choice.

Harry Briggs, a top venture capitalist, said, "If you just want to pursue something you enjoy, that might be a sign of laziness rather than genuine passion." Billionaire investor and *Shark Tank* star Mark Cuban agrees. "What a bunch of B.S. 'Follow your passion' is easily the worst advice you could ever give or get."

If you start with passion, you may never experience true fulfillment. That's because pursuing passion alone is like pursuing goals alone. You end up with your ladder on the wrong wall. But if you put your passion in context of what you are good at, you will experience true fulfillment. That's how you leverage your purpose to help others.

Just like you can't start with passion, you can't rely on passion either.

Passion is like fire. It can fuel positive change or destroy a person and the world around them.

The scholars during Galileo's time were passionate that the world was flat, but they were wrong. Adolf Hitler was passionate that his race was superior, but he was wrong. The builders of the *Titanic* were passionate that their ship was unsinkable, but they were wrong.

Let's consider a question that Stanford researchers asked students in 2018: Is passion fixed, or does it grow over time?

In this study, researchers looked at two groups of people. The first group believed that you are born with your passion, and it doesn't change. It's fixed. The second group believed that passion grows over time.

The first group that felt passion doesn't change were more likely to give up when things got hard. Why? Because, in their mind, doing something they are passionate about should be easy. Their belief was, if it isn't easy, it probably isn't their passion. The second group that believed passion can grow over time were more likely to push through setbacks and disappointments to achieve their goals. The researchers concluded, "Urging people to find their passion may lead them to put all their eggs in one basket, but then to drop that basket when it becomes difficult to carry."

In other words, building your life around passion alone is dangerous. You will jump from experience to experience and thrill to thrill, looking for something to excite you. When you finally find what you're passionate about, and the fuzzy feelings fade, you'll move on.

Passion is not an interest. Passion is not a hobby. Passion is something that pulls you. When properly identified and given the time to grow, it inspires you. It drives you to do better, grow faster, and live longer. Passion alone isn't purpose, but Pull-Passion is one of the four elements in your Purpose Factor. We will show you how to find your Pull-Passion, and how to use it, later in the book.

Passion Grows Over Time

On the journey to figuring out what's next, you cannot start with passion. That's because passion grows as you grow.

Successful people don't start with passion. They start with who they are and who they can help.

Walt Disney became passionate about entertaining children everywhere, but that's not where he started. As a young man, Walt had a Natural Advantage in starting projects and dreaming big. Despite his interests in drawing, he needed to grow his skills in illustration and business.

It took him five years to grow those skills and come up with the one and only Mickey Mouse. As his skills grew, his true passion grew, and from there, Walt developed the vision for Disneyland. He got that vision in the 1930s but didn't purchase the property until 1953. It wasn't passion alone that created Walt Disney's Disneyland. It was passion grown in context of his Purpose Factor that turned a young man's dream into a global sensation.

As the illustration shows, passion grows as you grow. As you develop your skills, you get better at your work. As you improve your abilities, you can help more people. And the more people

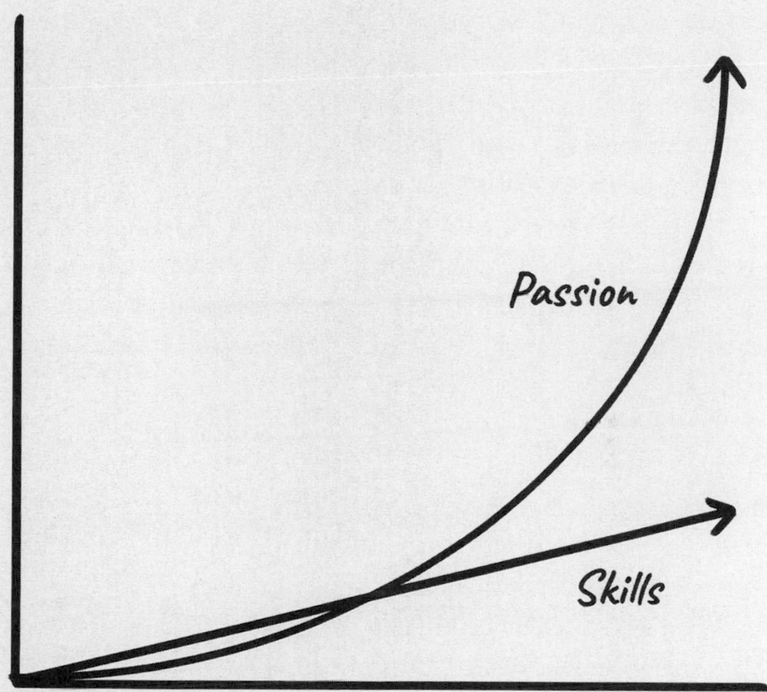

you help experience a transformation, the more passionate you become about your work.

On his show *Dirty Jobs*, Mike Rowe sat down with a very successful septic tank cleaner. The man was making millions doing what most of us would never do. He said:

> *"I looked around to see where everyone else was headed, and then I went the opposite way. Then I got good at my work. Then I began to prosper. Then one day, I realized I was passionate about other people's crap."*

In other words, passion may not exist at the start, but it will come with time.

Mike later explained in an interview, "When it comes to pursuing your hobby, by all means, let your passion lead you. But when it comes to making a living, it's easy to forget the dirty truth. Just because you're passionate about something, doesn't mean you won't suck at it."

Here's the truth: the more you grow your skills, and the more you focus on your Natural Advantage, the more likely you are to discover and pursue your true passion. We should stop telling people to pursue their passion and start telling them to develop it.

What Steve Said

The late Steve Jobs was considered one of the most determined entrepreneurs in the world. Some would describe his controversial leadership style, dramatic product rollouts, and obsession with excellence as "passion." They could even point to a commencement speech he gave in 2005:

> *"You've got to find what you love... The only way to do great work is to love what you do. If you haven't found it yet, keep looking. Don't settle. As with all matters of the heart, you'll know when you find it. And, like any great relationship, it just gets better and better as the years roll on."*

He said it in one speech, and everyone assumes its meaning. Don't do anything unless you're passionate. But perhaps he was saying something else. Perhaps he wasn't justifying twenty-five-year-olds turning down good jobs or mid-level leaders quitting because they don't love their work. Perhaps he was encouraging a journey of passion discovery.

This is the argument that Cal Newport makes in his book *So Good They Can't Ignore You*, and we agree. Steve Jobs wouldn't have started Apple if he had followed his own advice. In the beginning, Steve wasn't passionate about technology. He wanted to sell an idea, one that would give the customer a personal computer and a world-class experience. Apple isn't just a group of programmers passionate about coding. It is a structured business with a plan and process to execute its purpose.

Yes, great companies and great leaders are passionate. However, it isn't what they're building that gets them going. It's who they're helping and the world they're changing. They are passionate about using what they have to help others.

6

Fulfilling My Duties

"Not for ourselves alone are we born." —***Cicero***

Is your duty your purpose?

The first time Suzanne Watson went to medical school, she had a nine-month-old and another baby on the way. One week into classes, she quit. Balancing being a wife, a mother, and a medical student was just too much.

Suzanne and her husband agreed she would stay home with the kids and create a stable environment for her family. But Suzanne wanted more. She waited a few years and became an Episcopal priest, working at a church part-time. Not long after she became ordained, her husband committed suicide.

With her husband gone, Suzanne threw herself into working full-time to take care of her home and kids. The stay-at-home mom became a full-time working mother of four. The goals of "balance" and "stability" were gone. Years went by, and her kids grew up. At fifty years old, she began thinking about the time she had left. Her dream of becoming a doctor was still there. In the *Washington Post*, Suzanne wrote that her son threw down a challenge. He said, "You know, I've heard you talk about this your entire life, and you either need to do it now and sign up tomorrow, or you need to just shut up about it."

Parents often encourage their kids to pursue their dreams while putting their own dreams on hold. Suzanne had done just that until her son flipped the script. His message was clear. Stop talking about it, and just do it.

More than two decades after being accepted into medical school the first time, Suzanne was once again back in the classroom. When she walked into class on the first day, the room got quiet. The other students thought she was a professor. When she showed up at student parties, the partygoers thought she was a neighbor complaining about the noise. Suzanne may not look like the other students, but she works just as hard as they do. Maybe harder.

As of 2019, Suzanne is well into her residency, working on two specialties: family medicine and psychiatry. Motivated by her Origin Story of losing her husband to suicide, she intends to practice medicine in remote locations—where suicide rates are higher. After doing what she was "supposed to do" for more than twenty years, Suzanne is now doing what she was created to do. Full-time work isn't "work" anymore. It's a full-time purpose. It's full-time helping others with what's inside of her.

A false idea exists that we must set aside living out our purpose to take care of ourselves and our families, creating conflict between our purpose and a life event goal. It is either purpose or keeping a roof over my head. Purpose or my marriage. Purpose or my kids. Purpose or saving for retirement. It seems noble, wise, and even heroic to set aside our purpose to do what is expected of us.

The idea that you must choose responsibility over purpose is a myth. You can live out your purpose and be a good spouse, take care of your aging parents, and get out of debt. The right word is "and," not "or."

Of course, we need to take care of ourselves and our families. That is the minimum requirement. **But when we elevate that duty above our purpose, we let life's minimum requirements limit our maximum impact.**

To simply care for your household is not enough. It's playing small. It's neglecting your purpose. Worse, it's showing yourself and your family that purpose is not compatible with life.

The Martyr Complex

In a September 1972 edition of the *American Journal of Nursing*, Ruth Wibking wrote a letter to the editor. Ruth had read an article from the journal about nurses who suffer from martyr complex, the feeling that one must sacrifice so others can be saved. The article hit home for Ruth, who explained in her letter that nurses were expected to do more than ever before. As a result, their exhaustion was causing the quality of patient care to go down. But despite their exhaustion, they worked anyway—as any good martyr does. It got so bad that one evening Ruth did the unspeakable. She walked off duty in the middle of a shift. She writes, "I decided that I could no longer jeopardize patients' lives and that in walking off duty, I might call attention to the gross lack of nursing care." When she walked off that nursing floor, she was showing her fellow nurses, the hospital, and even us today that sacrificing well-being doesn't save lives; it risks lives.

In 1953, Emma Reinhardt wanted to know the impact of the martyr complex on the teaching profession. A teacher herself, Emma was curious if a student's view of teachers impacts their decision to become teachers themselves. It turns out it does. Emma conducted a study of 105 college students by asking them questions about their kindergarten through twelfth-grade teachers. Those who felt their teachers exhibited a martyr complex were less likely to become teachers. In other words, while the students appreciated their teachers' sacrifice, they didn't respect the sacrifice enough to replicate it.

We Mirror What Is Modeled

Would you tell your children not to follow their dreams? Would you encourage your friends to remain in a lousy job for years? Would you advise your family members to endure misery for decades in hopes of a happy retirement? Of course not.

When we set aside our purpose to fulfill duties and responsibilities, our actions tell others that purpose isn't worth pursuing. It's an afterthought—a back-burner idea. And if you believe it's okay to put off discovering your purpose, others, like your kids, might too. But if you model self-respect and using your purpose to help others, they will too.

But according to a study led by Dr. Kathleen McGinn of Harvard Business School, you don't have to put off anything. Dr. McGinn and her team wanted to see if female children are happier if their mothers worked or their mothers stayed at home. The study found that not only do daughters of working moms perform better in the workplace, but they're also just as happy as daughters of stay-at-home moms.

Reflecting on the results, Dr. McGinn said:

> *Having an employed mom makes daughters think that employment is compatible with parenting. If you're actually observing an employed mom manage a complex life and handle multiple demands—a job, a family, a household—you see that it can work. Everything we know about role models and social learning suggests that children are actively picking up life skills from the adults around them. It's all about what they're exposed to as children.*

In other words, we mirror what is modeled.

What if we told you we secretly filmed you last week. It would be for science, so it isn't creepy. And this is theoretical, so please don't sue us. But let's say we took the footage of your previous week and projected it on a giant screen. What would your routine and your actions say about your priorities? If you were to show the replay to your kids, friends, or colleagues, would they say your life is more about "taking care of your duties" or "using your purpose to help others?"

Put another way, what are you modeling for others?

Actions, more than words, demonstrate our real priorities. We may say we can't pursue our purpose because we have to get our kids through college. We may say that we don't have time to talk about purpose because we're too busy at work. But often, **our actions suggest that what was a short-term strategy to get by became a long-term lifestyle.**

Here's the typical life cycle for someone who continually puts off discovering their Purpose Factor, using it to help others, and experiencing maximum fulfillment.

- During High School—Doesn't know their purpose, but says, "I have to focus on getting good grades so I can get into college."
- During College—Still doesn't know their purpose, but says, "I have to focus on getting my degree to get a good job."
- After College—Still doesn't know their purpose, but says, "I don't have time because I'm too busy with my job (the one I don't like)."
- After Getting Married—Still doesn't know their purpose, but says, "We have to focus on settling down, buying a house, and starting a life together."
- After Having Kids—Still doesn't know their purpose, but says, "I have to focus on raising my kids and getting them through college."

- Empty Nester—Still doesn't know their purpose, but says, "It's too late for me. I have to keep this job (that I don't like) so that I have enough for retirement."
- Mid-Life Questioning—Still doesn't know their purpose, but wonders, "Have I wasted my time? Is there more to life than earning money and taking care of a home?"
- End-of-Life Reflection—Never found their purpose and thinks, "I'm thankful for my family, but I can't help but regret how I spent my time, that I never took the time to find my purpose, live it out to help others, and experience maximum fulfillment."

It can be sobering to consider where you are on life's timeline. But there's something beautiful about purpose. It's never too late to discover it and use it to help others.

Remember, your duty to yourself and your family is the minimum, but discovering your Purpose Factor and using it to help others is the maximum. You're meant for more than the minimum.

Should, Supposed To, and Have To

Language is powerful. We use it to express ourselves and understand others. On the other hand, we can use language to trick ourselves into believing things that aren't true. There are some fascinating phrases that we use to justify why we don't pursue our purpose. Inevitably the words *should*, *supposed to*, and *have to* come up.

Though similar in definition, they are distinct in usage. You *should* get good grades. You're *supposed to* go to college. You *have to* graduate on time. You *should* find love. You're *supposed to* get married. You *have to* have a perfect marriage. You *should* provide for yourself. You're *supposed to* get a job. You *have to* make a lot of money. It's as if we are saying we must do these things to the exclusion of everything else, especially our purpose.

2016 was a crazy year for us. We were juggling two companies, traveling weekly for clients, and speaking around the country. At that point, we were due for a vacation. Just before we left for Mexico, Gabrielle was asked to be a guest on a Chicago television program via Skype. Without hesitating, she agreed.

There was one problem. Our resort had terrible Wi-Fi and zero cell service. Now Gabrielle could have said, "Let's reschedule for another date," or, "I can't do it, but here's someone who can," or simply given a polite "No, but thank you for thinking of me." But she felt that she *had to* do the interview.

We returned from the pool with enough time to rearrange the room, fix her appearance, and check the lighting. Despite all of the preparation, it was a disaster. The signal was choppy, and the whole thing made her look unprofessional. Gabrielle didn't want to disappoint others by turning down the interview, but something worse happened. She embarrassed the hosts and herself, and she never got invited back. Gabrielle let her idea of *have to* get in the way of her impact.

Here's the truth: You don't *have to* do anything. You're in charge. It's your destiny. Yes, take care of yourself and your family, but also discover your Purpose Factor and live it out to help others.

Brian recently had a conversation with his friend Kyle, who was frustrated at work. Kyle enjoyed work most days but wondered if there was more to life. The conversation turned from talking about his job to finding Kyle's purpose.

Brian: What do you believe your purpose is?

Kyle: To provide for my family and be a good dad.

Brian: What was your purpose before you were a dad?

Kyle: To provide for my wife and make sure we have a good life.

Brian: So the basic definition of purpose is "the reason for which someone or something exists." Is your reason for existing to provide for your wife?

Kyle: Well, no. I don't think it's only that.

Brian: Okay. What else could it be? How do you provide for her?

Kyle: Make money, I guess. Keep a good, stable job.

Brian: So, make money? Is that your purpose?

Kyle: Well, no.

Brian: But you just said that your purpose was to provide for your wife and family. You do that by making money. How is your purpose not to make money?

Logic like this is why many of us stay in bad jobs and pursue the wrong priorities. We believe we have to out of a sense of duty, but in reality, we're only living to make a living. Oddly enough, Kyle represented himself as someone who felt it was wrong to make life all about earning money. It turned out he was pursuing money above purpose all along.

Perhaps you believe your purpose is about taking care of your family. Does that mean you didn't have a purpose before you had kids or got married? Maybe you believe your purpose is wrapped up in your job. Did you not have a purpose before you got this position? What would happen to your purpose if you were laid off tomorrow? Your Purpose Factor isn't about one thing or one person. It is what you have to help others. Your purpose gives you the right perspective, no matter your personal or professional situation. No matter your season, no matter your successes or setbacks, your Purpose Factor gives you clarity and specificity about who you are and how you can help others.

You have a duty to take care of yourself and your family. That's living at the minimum. You also have a duty to discover your purpose and use it to help others. That's living at the maximum. Where do you want to live? It's not duty or purpose. It's not purpose or duty. It's purpose *and* duty.

7

Finding Happiness

"Maybe happiness is something that we can only pursue, and maybe we can actually never have it." —***Chris Gardner***, The Pursuit of Happyness

Is the pursuit of happiness your purpose?

There is an eighteenth-century fable about a young African prince named Rasselas. He and his family reign over a place called Happy Valley, a perfect oasis in which every want and need is satisfied. As the prince, Rasselas spends his days preparing to take over as king but grows tired of waiting. Rasselas decides to escape Happy Valley with his sister, Princess Nekayah, and others in search of true happiness.

While on the journey, one of the group members, a housekeeper named Pekuah, is kidnapped, causing everyone to question the cost of their adventure. Princess Nekayah asks, "What is to be expected from our pursuit of happiness when we find the state of life to be such, that happiness itself is the cause of misery?"

What does it mean to be happy?

It's a big question and its answer has even bigger consequences. If you believe happiness is a certain income, then you will design a life around making money. If you believe happiness is health, you will design a life around well-being. If you believe happiness is family, you will design a life around those related to you. And if you believe happiness is about doing whatever feels good at the moment...well, you get the idea.

Our society is obsessed with happiness. We rank countries and cities "Most Happy" to "Least Happy." Start typing "How to be..." into a Google search bar, and the first suggested search will be "How to be happy." Hit enter and you'll get 9.7 billion search results. In the last couple of decades, mentions of the word *happy* in movies and books have gone up. Do you know what else has gone up? Diagnoses of major depression and anxiety in every age group.

Perhaps Princess Nekayah was onto something.

In ancient philosophy, happiness was the goal. According to philosophers like Aristotle, happiness was about balancing two things: pleasure and pursuit. Too much pleasure and your vices would kill you. Too much pursuit and your exertion would kill you. But for Aristotle and others, happiness wasn't about an experience or moment in time. Aristotle believed that happiness was only achieved at the end of your life—when you could fully account for your time and what you did with it. Or put another way, happiness was the result of living a life of purpose.

Why Happiness Won't Make You Happy

Dean Burnett describes himself as a neuroscientist and occasional comedian. He is fascinated with brain science and how it impacts the way we live and work. In an interview with the *Guardian* about his study of the human brain and happiness, Dean explains:

> *The thing that kept coming across was just how important other people are to your happiness. Your interactions with them, their approval, their empathy, your shame, your ambitions to be famous—it all depends on other people and their presence in our lives.*

Dean noticed a problem with happiness: it depends on what others do for us.

We're happy when someone lets us merge into traffic and unhappy when another cuts us off. We're happy when we close the deal but unhappy when we lose a contract to a competitor. We're happy on a first date and unhappy when someone cheats. We're happy when we look better than someone else but unhappy when they look better than we do.

In other words, if someone does us right, we're happy. If someone does us wrong, we're unhappy.

There's another problem with happiness. It's conditional. It's the flaky friend who says, "I'm on my way," but never shows up. So we tell ourselves, "If I get married, then I'll be happy." Or, "If I get that job, then I'll be happy." Perhaps, "When I move away from this town, then I'll be happy." Our obsession with happiness is making us miserable.

A very interesting set of studies shows the more we want to be happy, the less happy we end up being. In 2011, a group of researchers wanted to know if people who value happiness are the happiest. Ahead of the study, they predicted that "valuing happiness could be self-defeating because the more people value happiness, the more likely they will feel disappointed." Their prediction was right.

In the first study, participants who valued happiness the most reported lower levels of happiness in mildly stressful scenarios. Basically, they were more unhappy when little things went wrong. In the second study, participants who valued happiness were exposed to a happy scenario. And guess what? They responded less positively than those who didn't value happiness. Translation: people obsessed with happiness will be disappointed when things go wrong and disappointed when things go right.

The principle is clear: **if you want to be happy, don't focus on being happy.**

Hardwired for Happiness

When you ask a class of kindergarteners what they want to be when they grow up, you get all kinds of responses. "I want to be a firefighter!" or "I want to be a doctor!" or "I want to be an astronaut." Do you know what you never hear? The five-year-olds never scream out, "I just want to be happy!"

Yet, from adults, we hear something different. When we ask adults what they want, we hear "Honestly, I just want to be happy." From childhood to adulthood, people go from wanting to *be* something to wanting to *feel* something.

When we say we just want to be happy, we are really saying something else. We just don't want to hurt anymore. We just don't want to be in debt anymore. We just don't want to feel disappointed anymore. We have made happiness the avoidance of pain instead of an abundance of goodness.

We have stopped dreaming, stopped striving, and now just want to feel better. Happiness is not the antidote to pain. It will not remove regret or redeem mistakes. Purpose is the only thing that can do that.

The Pursuit of Purpose

There are two rules of happiness.

Dan Gilbert is a professor at Harvard and an expert on decision-making. Dan wanted to see if there is a connection between decision-making and happiness. To do so, he conducted a study with students interested in learning photography. The students were taught how to adjust the focus of the camera, place the subject in the frame, and print the photos. To prove their mastery of the content, they were instructed to take photos of two things that have deep meaning to them and then process the photos.

After the photos were presented to the students, they were then told that they could keep only one. The other was to be kept as proof of their participation in the class and they would never see it again. But that's not all. Dan wanted to see if being forced to make a choice immediately impacted the students' happiness. Half of the students were told that they had to make the decision now. The other group was told they had to make a decision now, but they could come back and exchange the photo at any point in the next few days.

The results? The students who were told they had to choose a photo with no option to switch reported being twice as satisfied with their choice as the students who were given the option to switch out. It seems the more choices we believe we have, the more dissatisfied we are with what we currently have.

This brings us to our first rule of happiness: **happiness is not about having what you want, but about wanting what you have.**

There is another famous Harvard study about money and happiness. In the study, participants were given an envelope that contained cash in the form of either five, fifteen, or twenty dollars. Before they could open the envelope to see which amount they got, participants were asked how happy they were. Their responses were recorded.

The participants were then split into two groups. One group was told to use the money to cover an expense or buy a gift for themselves. In other words, they could spend the money on whatever they wanted. The other group was told to spend the money on someone else. At the end of the day, the participants were again asked how happy they were. Not surprisingly, the group that gave their money away was far happier than the group that spent on themselves. Not only that, it seemed that the individuals who gave away five dollars were just as happy as the folks who gave away twenty.

So does money buy happiness? It sure does, but it only takes about five dollars.

An ancient Chinese proverb states:

If you want happiness for an hour, take a nap.
If you want happiness for a day, go fishing.
If you want happiness for a month, get married.
If you want happiness for a year, inherit a fortune.
If you want happiness for a lifetime, help somebody else.

Which leads to the second rule of happiness: **happiness isn't about getting what we want; it's about giving what we have.**

The Right Pursuit

Gabrielle was sitting across from Tim Goeglein in his office overlooking the Supreme Court. Tim was the former deputy director of the White House Office of Public Liaison under President George W. Bush. He had designed his entire life to get to the White House, and it worked.

To stay in touch with his Indiana roots, Tim started writing as an unpaid guest contributor for his hometown paper, the *Fort Wayne News-Sentinel*. Nancy Nall Derringer, a journalist formerly with the *News-Sentinel*, was reading one of Tim's 2008 articles when she noticed an unusual name, "Eugen Rosenstock-Huessy." She explains in her blog, "This name was so goofy, just for the

[heck] of it, I Googled it." Her search revealed a juicy story. Tim was plagiarizing his articles.

By noon the next day, twenty out of Tim's thirty-eight articles had been flagged. CNN picked up the story and Tim was out. He went from White House insider to political leper in less than twenty-four hours.

Now, years later, Tim is serving as the political liaison for a large nonprofit. He had survived his scandal, but barely. When asked about why he did it, he admitted that he felt like he needed to be more profound. He didn't believe that what he knew and what he did was enough. Tim thought the recognition of others would make him happy. But out of the limelight, Tim was happier than ever.

Sitting in his office, Tim explained that it's not the position that makes you happy. It's what you're doing with your life that brings joy.

In other words, it's about purpose, not happiness.

Now that you've overcome the bad beliefs holding you back, it's time to adopt new beliefs that will equip you to discover your Purpose Factor.

Purpose is what you have to help others.

Part Two

The Shift: The Powerful Truths That Change Everything

8

The Oxygen Mask Principle

From books to superhero movies, we love stories of extreme sacrifice. In everyday life, we hold doors for others, offer guests the last piece of pie, and teach children that it's better to give than receive. Though it's nice to be nice, being selfless isn't always good, and being selfish isn't always bad.

In the 1999 cult classic movie *Fight Club*, Edward Norton's character (the narrator who remains unnamed the whole film) is seated on an airplane next to Tyler Durden, played by Brad Pitt. In the middle of a sarcastic discussion about the responsibilities of sitting in the exit row, Tyler asks, "You know why they put oxygen masks on planes?"

Edward's character responds, "So they can breathe?"

Shaking his head no, Tyler says, "Oxygen gets you high. In a catastrophic emergency, you're taking giant panicked breaths. Suddenly you become euphoric, docile. You accept your fate.... It's all right here," as he points at the plane's emergency instruction manual. "Emergency water landing. Six hundred miles an hour. Blank faces, calm as Hindu cows."

The Oxygen Mask Principle

It turns out Tyler is wrong. It's the lack of oxygen that causes euphoria. Under normal circumstances, a pressurized cabin protects you from the lack of oxygen outside the plane. If the cabin suddenly depressurizes, the oxygen masks provide passengers with up to fifteen minutes of oxygen. That's long enough for the pilots to get the plane back to a safe altitude. The masks protect you from what a lack of oxygen can do to you, such as brain damage or death.

So what's it like to be in a depressurized airplane? We came across a story from a woman named Tracey Bryan. In the early 1990s, Tracey was on a Royal Australian Air Force flight. The pilot came over the system to make a routine announcement. He stopped mid-sentence. The plane immediately began a rapid descent. It was the kind of descent you could expect on a theme park roller coaster, not a routine flight home. Tracey looked outside the window of the airplane to see the aircraft's wings bending at an alarming angle.

Tracey was not a calm flier, but in this moment, she wasn't anxious. Interestingly, when the oxygen masks dropped from the ceiling, she teased her colleagues for putting them on. She was convinced that the masks fell by mistake even though it was clear that they didn't. The aircraft had experienced a sudden decompression. Tracey was calm because she was suffering from hypoxia, a lack of oxygen to the body, which causes euphoria. Her seatmate shoved an oxygen mask on her face, and the hypoxia subsided.

The plane stabilized, and Tracey could think clearly again.

How many times have you heard the safety brief at the beginning of a flight? The flight attendant says, "Place the mask over your nose and mouth. Secure your mask before helping others." The message is simple. If you can't breathe, you can't help yourself or others. Attend to yourself or it could cost you your life or someone else's.

In the last section, we addressed the myths that we believe about purpose. We showed you how they have led us astray and kept us from using our purpose to help others. In this section, we will show you how to replace those bad beliefs about purpose with good beliefs that will help you live a more meaningful and impactful life.

There are three beliefs you must adopt before discovering your purpose. This is the first belief to adopt: **You first, others second.**

There's an ancient teaching that warns against helping others before helping ourselves. It says, "Don't point out the speck in your neighbor's eye when you have a log in your own." When we focus on helping others before discovering our Purpose Factor, we can't see clearly. If you can't see clearly, you can't help others—with or without specks in our eyes.

Our friend's mom had a stroke. No one saw it coming. She was strong and happy with one of those smiles you can't forget. She volunteered at church and was active in her community. In a moment, everything changed. One day she was delivering meals to the needy, and the next, she was unable to walk or speak. Her entire life had been about taking care of her family and community, but she hadn't taken care of herself.

Two years after her stroke, she had regained the ability to speak but was still working on her mobility. In a conversation with her daughter, she said she was thankful for what happened. Before the stroke, she remembered her kids telling her, "Slow down, take care of yourself, and go on vacation," but she never did. Her extreme selflessness on the outside wore her down on the inside. If you go long enough without your oxygen mask, life will force you to put it on anyway.

The Myth of Self-Care

We live in a time in which "self-care" is celebrated. A quick search on self-care reveals headlines like "5 Ways to Take a Mental Health Day for Cheap," "Bring a Yoga Mat and an Open

Mind. Goats are Provided," or "Take a Day Off, You Deserve It." Well-being initiatives at companies and universities are on the rise. The self-help industry rakes in more than $9 billion annually. But self-care and self-help aren't the enemy. It all depends on how you use them.

When it comes to self-care and your purpose, think of yourself as a water pitcher. The purpose of a pitcher is to store water and serve it as needed. If you keep the pitcher full, it can be used to help others. If it remains empty, it isn't serving its purpose. Finding and using your Purpose Factor is how you keep your water pitcher full.

Researchers studied what happens when hospital nurses take care of others, but not themselves. The study observed more than seventy-four thousand nurses over twenty-two years. It showed that nurses who worked night shifts were more likely to smoke, be overweight, and have diabetes and hypertension as well as a higher risk of dying from cancer. These nurses were taking care of others, but not themselves—and it was killing them. There's nothing noble about using what's in your pitcher to help others without first taking care of yourself. You can't help others if you're not here.

Believe You Are Worth It

Before you can adopt the belief of "You first, others second," you must believe that you're worth it. When real estate developers are deciding whether to renovate or tear down an old building, they must determine whether the building is worth it. If so, then they'll renovate. If not, they'll tear the building down and start over.

Do you believe that you're worth it?

When people avoid discovering their Purpose Factor, they've made up their minds. They're not worth it. They don't say it like that. But they say things like, "I'm too old to change now," or "If I haven't found it yet, I probably never will," or "My life's pretty good as it is." Translation: "My purpose isn't worth changing for." If you believe that you're too far gone, too old, or that the change will be too hard, you will not change. But if you recognize, like we do, that your life changes the moment you discover your Purpose Factor, the change will be faster and easier than you expect.

So can you change the way you view yourself?

A group of psychologists wanted to know if people could act themselves into higher self-esteem. So what did they do? First, they had participants rate their current level of self-esteem. Next, they asked participants to write down four important chapters in their life. This could be moving as a child, graduating from college debt-free, or being promoted. Finally, participants were told to rate their level of self-esteem after the experiment. Not only did participants report feeling more confident, but they felt they understood themselves better. Reflecting on their ability to overcome past setbacks and achieve a goal increased their self confidence in the present. Perhaps the key to changing how we view ourselves is changing what we believe about ourselves.

For every excuse, we've got a story to destroy it. If you feel you're too far gone, we've seen a young man go from homeless to competing in national barbering competitions. If you think you're too old, we've seen a seventy-four-year-old woman write her first book in thirteen days after sitting on the idea for twenty years. If you feel that change is too hard, we've seen an event planner leave her job and go on to consult parliaments and run a major program at the United Nations.

You are far more valuable than you believe. Like a developer deciding to keep the building or tear it down, you have to believe that you are worth the renovation. You may need to tear down some walls by dealing with the past. You may need a new foundation of purpose, but it's worth it because you are worth it. Before you can help others, you have to help yourself.

If you're always selfless, you'll never know your purpose. If you're always selfish, you'll never help others with what's inside of you. Be selfish enough to find your Purpose Factor and be selfless enough to help others with it.

9

Choose Your Crisis Before Your Crisis Chooses You

It was the final segment of the *Jeopardy!* "Tournament of Champions." When the show's host, Alex Trebek, went to read Dhruv Guar's answer, he started to cry. Dhruv had wagered all but five dollars of his earnings on the answer "What is we [heart] you, Alex!"

Dhruv's unconventional answer was in response to the game show host's recent announcement that he had stage four pancreatic cancer.

In a December 2019 interview with ABC News, Alex shared:

> *I have learned something the past year, and it's this: We don't know when we're going to die. Because of the cancer diagnosis, it's no longer an open-ended life, it's a closed-ended life because of the terrible survival rates of pancreatic cancer.*

Most of us don't often consider our mortality. We don't think about how much time we've wasted, how many mistakes we've made, or how much longer we have on this planet. But what Alex said is true. Life is "closed-ended."

When we're young, life feels open-ended. It feels like there are endless possibilities. We feel that anything can happen. But no matter our age, we are all on a timeline, and we will face our end. So what do we do with the time we have?

The Seven-to-One Rule

Brian's grandmother passed away in 2019 after a long battle with Parkinson's disease. Preparing to give the eulogy, Brian reflected on his grandmother's life and how quickly our days go by. To keep himself accountable, he created a "Life Clock." Brian's Life Clock is a simple calculation that takes the average age a man will live to and counts backward. Every day it ticks away, reminding him to use his Purpose Factor.

Considering our mortality can feel unnerving, but it can also be an accountability tool. If you believe you have fifty years to use your purpose, you may prioritize it differently than folks who believe they have less time. Feeling that you have less time may make you more motivated to find your purpose today. No matter how much is left on your Life Clock, you can choose to make purpose a priority.

Herein lies the second belief you must adopt before finding your purpose: **Choose your crisis before your crisis chooses you.**

The first belief you must adopt, "You first, others second," changes the way you prioritize finding your purpose. The second belief, "Choose your crisis before your crisis chooses you," puts you back in control of finding your purpose.

So can we ask you a question? How are you using your time?

In the developed world, the average life expectancy is seventy-eight years. The first two decades of our lives are spent growing up and learning how to work and live. Around age twenty, we start contributing to society. We go to school, get a job, start families, and become accountable for ourselves. The average retirement age is sixty-two years old, but that doesn't mean we stop contributing. We once heard a terrible joke from one of our older clients. He explained, "I'm not going to retire. I'm going to retread." We don't stop contributing when we stop working. We stop contributing when we stop breathing. If you still have oxygen in your lungs, you aren't finished helping the world around you. Oxygen equals purpose.

Therefore, if each of us lives to the average age of seventy-eight, we have fifty-eight productive years. That's fifty-eight years to use your Purpose Factor to help others with what you have.

To put that in perspective, it only takes seven months to live 1 percent of your productive life. That's seven to one. Seven months. One percent.

Every seven months, you lose 1 percent of the time you have to help others. Consider your last seven months. What did you achieve? What are you most proud of? How much closer are you to your goals?

We know that a lot can happen in seven months. You can go from unemployment to full employment. You can go from frustrated with your love life to head-over-heels in love. You can go from unhealthy and sluggish to active and thriving.

On the other hand, seven months can fly by in a flash. Months, years, even decades start to run together as the demands of life eat away your time. But it isn't just the duties of life that keeps us busy. It's the useless stuff too. In 2016 the average American adult watched about five hours of television per day. That's seventy-six days a year consuming media. With those numbers, Americans will spend 4,180 days watching television during their fifty-five productive years. That's 23 percent of a productive life spent watching television.

When seven months is 1 percent of the time you have to help others, you stop acting as if life is open-ended and start considering how to use the time you have left.

"This Is a Crisis!"

The best time to look for a new job is while you still have one. The best time to deal with your health is while you're still healthy. The best time to go grocery shopping is when you're not hungry. We know that we don't make the best decisions in times of crisis, yet we continue to put ourselves in the same position again and again.

Research shows we put off making important decisions because we're afraid of what might happen. We think, "What if I'm wrong? What if it doesn't work out? What will others think of me?" Instead of taking action, we let our circumstances decide for us. And our circumstances usually don't decide in our favor.

The same thing happens when it comes to discovering our Purpose Factor. We put it off. The voice in our head says there's got to be more to life than waking up, going to work, coming home, going to bed, and starting all over again. But we ignore the voice and wait for our crisis of purpose to arrive. The truth is, we will all face a crisis of purpose. It may be when you're young or when you're older. It may happen in the middle of your happiest day or saddest day, but one thing is true: at some point in your life, you'll wonder why you're here and what to do about it.

Crises have a funny way of getting our attention. Challenging times eliminate comfort and force us to consider the uncomfortable. Losing a job takes away a steady income, and we ask, "What's my purpose outside my job?" Losing a loved one takes away connectedness and companionship, and we question, "What's my purpose beyond my family and friends?" A failure tears down our self-confidence, and we wonder, "Will I ever get back up?"

Successful people address the crisis before it becomes a crisis.

"Choose the Suck"

In every crisis, there's a common theme. A crisis makes us feel out of control. One day, everything is normal and predictable. The next, it's chaotic and uncertain. While you can't control what life will throw at you, you can control how you think, act, and react. And the more you can control your reaction, the less severe the crisis ends up being.

In 2017, a group of researchers studied fifty people and their responses to pain. The researchers wanted to know if people who have a sense of control over physical pain feel less pain than those who don't have a sense of control.

The process was simple. In the first experiment, the participants were seated in front of a computer. At random, either a hot laser or a light electrical current would be applied to their left hand. Afterward, the participants were told to rate their level of pain.

In the second experiment, the participants were given two buttons. They were told both buttons would cause physical discomfort, but one was more painful than the other. Unlike the first experiment, the participants could choose which button to press and when. Again, the participants were asked to rate their pain levels. In the end, when given the ability to control their experience, the participants reported feeling less pain.

Another study looked at the relationship between having a sense of purpose in life and chronic pain in patients. Researchers found that patients who "have a reason for living are often more able to tolerate pain and maintain function." Even when dealing with pain, the Purpose Factor prevails.

Both of these studies show that you feel more pain when you're not in control and less pain when you're in control. If you wait to discover your purpose, you'll continue feeling out of control. You'll deal with more frustration, more failure, and more regret. If you choose to discover your Purpose Factor and use it to help others, you'll be in control of your life and your legacy.

Doug Bopst knows the power behind choosing your crisis. From a young age, Doug suffered from anxiety and depression. He did drugs, dealt drugs, and subsequently landed in prison by age twenty-one. Doug had little reason to live or change. That was until his fitness fanatic cellmate challenged him to stop making excuses and finally get in shape. At the time, Doug was fifty pounds overweight. He could barely do a push-up, but the idea of playing another game of Scrabble drove him crazy. To distract himself from his current situation, Doug decided to view the pain of working out as progress.

Doug knew all about pain. He was bullied as a kid and had a rocky relationship with his parents. He had abused drugs to the degree that he had burned a hole in his nose. But in prison, he chose the pain he could control instead of the pain he couldn't. Even when his body didn't want to do another push-up, he chose to embrace it. Today, that pain fuels his purpose. Now Doug is an award-winning fitness trainer and motivational speaker.

In an interview with *Impact Theory* host Tom Bilyeu, Doug said you have to choose your suck to get ahead. He also said that owning his life instead of blaming others changed his life. He explained, "We're not defined by our circumstances. We're defined by the choices we make in response to those circumstances."

The choice is clear. Choose your crisis before your crisis chooses you.

Alex Trebek joined *60 Minutes* to reflect on his career as the thirty-five-year host of *Jeopardy!* In the interview, Alex explained:

> *Throughout my life, I've always wondered about how courageous a human being I was. I just look at it as it's a part of life. Does that mean I'm courageous because I'm dealing with it? No. I could be scared to death and I'd still have to deal with it. But I'm not scared to death. So, maybe I am courageous.*

The most courageous among us will deal with their crisis before it knocks at the door. We were not courageous. Crisis forced us to discover our Purpose Factors, but that doesn't have to be you. You didn't choose your family. You can't control the weather, the economy, or what people think of you or do to you. But you can control yourself. If you wait for life to happen to you, it will. If you discover your Purpose Factor, life will happen because of you.

10

Comparison Kills Purpose

"Comparison is the thief of joy." —***Theodore Roosevelt***

Anna Delvey lived a lavish life as a New York socialite. The daughter of a German diplomat, Anna stayed at the best hotels, partied at the top clubs, and traveled around the world. Her social media accounts captured every expensive night out, designer dress, and celebrity selfie. The only problem? It was all a lie.

Anna was not a German heiress. Her father was a former truck driver and now owned a heating and air company. She did not have a trust fund; she was a thief. For ten months, the twenty-eight-year-old had deposited $15,000 in bad checks, lied to secure a $100,000 loan, and racked up over $275,000 of unpaid expenses. Anna was caught, imprisoned, and prosecuted.

In his opening statement, Anna's attorney defended her actions, saying his client was caught up in the New York lifestyle. The pressure to fit in pushed her to live by the motto, "Fake it until you make it." Her attorney argued that everything she did—the lies, theft, and betrayal—was for a good reason. The judge and jury didn't buy it. In October 2017, Anna was charged with six counts of larceny and grand larceny, sentenced to up to twelve years in prison, and threatened with deportation.

But during her trial, there was a powerful moment. As the sides wrapped up their arguments, Anna's attorney explained, "There's a little bit of Anna in all of us." In other words, we all want what we don't have.

The Science of Comparison

Here is the third and final belief to adopt: **comparison kills purpose**.

Comparison is wanting what others have or what they pretend to have.

Comparison is nothing new. There's a reason that "Do not covet" is part of the Ten Commandments. But now we compare faster than ever. Before social media, we heard about what others were doing from the newspaper or family gossip; "Did you hear that Bill's daughter is going to Harvard?" and "Did you see that Hannah just bought that house?"

Now with a few clicks and swipes, we are instantly exposed to the highlight reel of others' lives. You see your old college friend on a glamorous European vacation. You wonder, "Didn't she just go to Bali a few months ago?" You keep scrolling and see an update from a former colleague. He announces that he got a big promotion, he is engaged to a model, and he is moving to Chicago. You roll your eyes and jump on another pointless conference call. Social media allows us to compare our present reality to the carefully constructed reality of others.

Social media accounts can be manipulated to make you appear more successful, more happy, and more connected than you really are, yet we give social media and its influencers more power than they deserve.

Comparison is not new or exclusive to social media. In 1984, researchers wanted to measure the impact of comparison among undergraduate students. They had the participants take a simple personality test. After reviewing their results, participants were told about another person who did better on the test. The participants were asked how they felt about that person. The results?

Participants were more jealous and less trusting of the person who did well. Not only that, they were more likely to disparage them and avoid friendship with that person. Why does this matter? Because the test and the results were made up. Participants were randomly assigned fake test results and then asked to compare themselves against another person whose results were fake as well.

Do you see the implication? Social media followers. Brand names. Lunch appointments. Deals closed. Comparison keeps score of things that don't matter on a scoreboard that doesn't matter.

What (And Who) We Compare To

There are three types of comparison keeping you from living out your purpose. Each of them is equally tempting and equally dangerous to your purpose.

1. Comparison to the Past

When Gabrielle was in middle school, she would borrow clothes from her older sister's much cooler wardrobe without asking. So they made a deal: Gabrielle would do her sister's reading homework in exchange for one article of clothing. That deal was how Gabrielle first read *The Great Gatsby*.

The premise of the book is simple. Jay Gatsby, a self-made millionaire, tries to use his fortune to win back his young love, Daisy. Nick Carraway, the narrator, is Jay's neighbor and Daisy's cousin. In one memorable scene, Jay is discussing his plan to get Daisy back with Nick. As Nick and Jay walk home from one of Gatsby's lavish parties, Nick tries to talk sense to his friend.

Nick: "You can't repeat the past."

Jay: "Can't repeat the past? Why, of course you can!"

Jay Gatsby refused to move on with his life because he was comparing his present to his past. Maybe there is a little bit of Gatsby in us too. We believe we can relive the past when we compare our today to our yesterday. When we do, we don't allow ourselves to be content in the present. We say things like "Things were easier at my last job," or "Life was less complicated when I was single," or "Our last neighborhood was better."

Comparing your present with your past is dangerous if you want to live out your Purpose Factor. Why? Because purpose is future-focused and forward-moving. Your Purpose Factor is what you have to help others now, not what you missed in the past. **You can't be fulfilled today if you keep looking back at yesterday.**

2. Comparison to Others

Mallory Knight didn't realize her struggle with comparison until she was pregnant with her son. As soon as she got pregnant, she sought out other moms for advice. Mallory scoured Google, mommy blogs, and social media groups to see what other people thought. Should she go back to work, stay at home, always swaddle, go organic? The information was overwhelming. In the midst of it all, comparison crept in. She noticed the strollers that other moms had, what their nurseries looked like, and how they were raising their kids. Everything she thought she wanted wasn't good enough anymore.

Mallory became overwhelmed by comparison. Her self-esteem plummeted. She bought more and more stuff to make it look like she was happy, but she wasn't. Mallory's husband intervened.

He helped her see that in pursuit of finding her identity as a mom, she had lost herself. She was letting other people, most of whom she had never met, define her life and her priorities.

We hear it all of the time.

"Everyone is getting married."

"Everyone is having kids."

"Everyone is retiring."

"Everyone is going on vacation."

Phrases like these are dangerous. They make us question who we are and wonder if what we have is enough. When you know your Purpose Factor and use it, you don't need to compare yourself to anyone. You know that you are enough.

We compare ourselves to the people who best reflect the lifestyle we want. We compare ourselves to other parents, other students, other women, and other men who remind us of what we don't have. Because our reality does not look like theirs, we assume that we are doing something wrong. The truth is, they are just as susceptible to comparison as we are! It is impossible to be content if you compare.

We also look at people who are farther along than we are. They have more social media followers, more clients, or more money. We don't think that we can compete or do well because someone else is already in that space. When we do that, we are comparing our Chapter One to their Chapter Fifty. Your journey is your own. Your purpose is your own. Your path and your impact are your own. Do not let comparison steal that from you. Comparison is how we end up using others as our standard instead of using our Purpose Factor as our standard.

You will never discover your Purpose Factor if you are too distracted comparing yourself to others. Comparison and purpose are not compatible. Comparison uses outside influences as a measuring stick. Purpose is all internal. Comparison is short-term. Purpose is long-term.

Comparison presents a false reality. Purpose presents the truth as to who you are and who you can help.

3. Comparison to Your Blueprint

Comparison requires a reference point. Without a reference point, there is no comparison. You are only considered short in comparison to someone who is tall. You're only regarded as poor in comparison to someone rich. Something is cheap in comparison to something that is expensive. You compare a sale price to the original price to determine if it's a good deal.

But for us, our reference point is the picture in our mind. It is the blueprint of what we thought our life would be today or what we thought our life should be tomorrow. The problem with the blueprint is that it often doesn't match our present reality.

That blueprint could tell you, "You aren't as far along as you should be." It could say to you, "You aren't as happy as you could be." Or even, "You aren't as fit as you should be."

In April 2013, Dove Beauty released a six-minute film on self-image. In the film, women are placed behind a white sheet and asked to explain their facial features. They describe their eyes, the shape of their nose, and the structure of their jaw. On the other side of the sheet, an FBI-trained forensic artist draws their appearance using only the subject's self-description. Later, those same women were described by individuals who had briefly met them to the same forensic artist. The artist produced separate portraits from the two descriptions and showed them to the women. The results were shocking.

The portraits done based on the women's self-perception were harsh and unflattering. The portraits done based on the perception of others were beautiful and more accurate. The women didn't realize how far off their mental blueprints were. Looking at the two portraits side by side, one woman said, "I've come a long way in how I see myself, but I think I have some way to go."

It is dangerous to trust a blueprint that is not accurate. It's worse when you let that blueprint distract you from your purpose.

When it comes to fixing the blueprint problem, you have two options. You can reframe your blueprint, or you can change your approach.

Reframing requires you to consider if your dreams, ideas, and goals are what they should be. If not, you need to adjust your blueprint to reflect your Purpose Factor. If your blueprint is accurate, then you need to change your approach.

You change your approach by adjusting your action to achieve your blueprint. The following questions help you reframe your approach to your blueprint. What daily habits do you need to get to your goal? What people do you need to cut out of your life? What kind of people do you need more of in your life? What must happen by when so that your blueprint is achieved?

The Antidote to Comparison

Comparison distracts you from finding and using your Purpose Factor to help others. When you are comparing, you are not asking the question "Who am I, and who can I help?" Instead you are asking the question "Who am I not, and why am I not like someone else?"

If comparison is the disease, your Purpose Factor is the antidote. When you know your Purpose Factor, you don't worry if someone is making more money than you. When you know how you can help others, you aren't concerned with how others have risen to fame or popularity. You are content in who you are because you know how you can help.

It was the 2016 Summer Olympics, and Michael Phelps was focused. The record-breaking American swimmer was going for another medal—this time in the 200-meter butterfly. South African Chad le Clos, one of Phelps's rivals, had beaten him in the 2008 London Olympics by 5 1/100ths of a second. Le Clos was back for more. Through each lap, the swimmers were neck and neck. Until the final lap, when Phelps began passing le Clos in the final sprint.

A now-famous photo captured a millisecond in time when le Clos was looking at Phelps. Phelps was eyes forward, focused on his goal of winning a gold medal. Phelps later admitted that it was the rivalry that drove him. Before the race, he told a reporter, "I'm going to let what I do in the pool do my talking." Phelps won the gold medal—his twentieth—and le Clos failed to make the medal stand. Phelps was driven to become his best. Le Clos was lost in his comparison.

When you free yourself from the grip of comparison, amazing things happen. Before, you saw roadblocks. Now you see opportunities. Before, you felt that you weren't enough. Now you feel confident. Before, you experienced discouragement. Now you experience fulfillment. Before, you followed after others. Now you lead yourself.

When you know your Purpose Factor, you stop looking at the past; you stop looking left and right. You know who you are and who you can help—and you can be proud of yourself and others. Perhaps Bob Goff, author of *Love Does*, said it best when he explained, "We won't be distracted by comparison if we are captivated with purpose."

Fulfillment is the result of helping others with your purpose.

Part Three

The Process: The Simple Path to Clarity

Introduction

When we were developing the Purpose Factor, we tested scores of iterations. Should we call it an equation? A secret? A method? A formula? We were close, but something was off. And then it hit us.

We asked ourselves, what do you call the one thing that makes the difference? The *factor*.

A factor is a single component that determines a result. A factor is the one thing that influences everything else. An economic factor influences the economy. A wind chill factor influences the weather. A numerical factor will influence the rest of an equation. Your purpose is the factor that, when understood and used, influences every area of your life. It influences how you work, how you live, and what you do.

There are three rules to finding your Purpose Factor: Be Specific. Be Honest. Take Ownership. When followed, these rules define the depth of your transformation. Follow these three rules and you will find your Purpose Factor.

The first rule you must follow to find your Purpose Factor is Be Specific. The more specific you are in defining each element of your Purpose Factor, the better your breakthrough. There are four elements of your Purpose Factor. To help you identify each element, we have developed a series of questions. Remember, general answers lead to general results and specific answers lead to specific results. The more specific you are with your purpose, the more specific you will be with your impact.

The key to getting great results is taking the time to get specific. If we help someone find their Purpose Factor and they don't get instant clarity, it is always because they didn't follow the rule of specificity.

But it is more than specificity. To discover your purpose, you must Be Honest with your answers. The questions we ask throughout this section are designed to reveal your Purpose Factor. The answers to those questions give you freedom and permission to live life to the fullest. Failing to give truthful answers only hurts you and limits how you can use your Purpose Factor. If you are not honest with yourself, you will not be able to help others with what you have.

Finally, the third rule to finding your Purpose Factor is Take Ownership. You must own the discovery and application of your Purpose Factor. No one will do that for you. Great leaders take responsibility for their successes and failures. They don't wait for others to act. They make the first move. They don't blame others for what happened in the past. They take ownership of their past, present, and future. You cannot find your Purpose Factor if you are too busy pointing fingers at others. Ownership is a crucial element to discovering and using your Purpose Factor.

Preparing for Transformation

You have eliminated bad beliefs. You have adopted new mindsets. Now it's time to find your Purpose Factor.

Natural Advantage + Acquired Skills + Pull Passion + Origin Story = Purpose Factor

In this section, you will discover your Purpose Factor. The Purpose Factor has four elements: Natural Advantage, Acquired Skills, Pull-Passion, and Origin Story.

Your Natural Advantage is the role you tend to play. It is what comes second nature to you. Your Acquired Skills are the abilities you developed through study or experience. Your Pull-Passion is the problem you want to solve in the world around you. Your Origin Story is the moment or series of moments that most shaped your perspective.

Combining Natural Advantage, Acquired Skills, Pull-Passion, and Origin Story will help you finally understand who you are and who you can help. By following the rules and taking each element one at a time, you will get extreme clarity on what matters most.

11

Your Natural Advantage

"Start where you are. Use what you have. Do what you can."
—Arthur Ashe

As we started to write this book, we were reading another book, *Bird by Bird*, by Anne Lamott. It's a humorous and honest account of the life of a writer. It wasn't the concept or content of the book that intrigued us. It was the title.

The title came from the author's childhood. While growing up, Anne's little brother was writing a book report about birds. She remembers her brother sitting at the kitchen table, overwhelmed by the task. That was until her father put his hand on her brother's shoulder and said, "Just take it bird by bird."

Discovering your purpose may not be a book report about birds, but one thing is true: the idea of finding your purpose can feel overwhelming. Questions like, "Who am I?" or "What am I supposed to do?" or "Where am I going next?" are daunting. And while they are questions that are worth answering, that doesn't make answering them any easier.

Until now, motivators have left purpose without meaning and made its discovery too complicated and emotional. But for you, discovering your purpose doesn't have to be that way. As you've seen by now, your Purpose Factor has four easy-to-understand elements. In this section, we're going to walk you through the discovery and the questions to ask yourself to identify each element of your Purpose Factor.

We're going to help you get specific about each element and how to use them in your situation. The next section will show you exactly how to combine the elements of your Purpose Factor to help others and experience maximum fulfillment.

We have thrown out the old definitions of purpose and taken on new mindsets. It's now time to discover your Purpose Factor.

The Best Place to Start Is at the Beginning

Before the gun goes off, runners line up at the start line. When you're making a recipe, you first look at the ingredients. When you read a book, you start with the first chapter. As Lewis Carroll, author of *Alice's Adventures in Wonderland*, said, "Begin at the beginning."

Your Natural Advantage is the starting point to answering the question, "Who am I, and who am I supposed to help?"

In the 2003 comedy *Anger Management*, Jack Nicholson plays Dr. Buddy Rydell, a therapist brought in to help Adam Sandler's character, Dave Buznik, overcome his personal issues. During a group therapy session, Dr. Rydell asks Dave, "Who are you?"

Dave, unsure of himself, responds, "Well, I'm an executive assistant at a major pet products company." Dr. Rydell interrupts and says, "Dave, I don't want you to tell us what you do. I want you to tell us who you are." Thrown off, Dave tries again, "Oh, all right. Um, I'm a pretty good guy. I, um, I like playing tennis on occasion, um...."

Dr. Rydell interrupts again, "Also, not your hobbies Dave. Just simple, just tell us who you are." Unsure of what Dr. Rydell is asking for, Dave says, "I just, maybe you could give me an example of what a good answer would be, um.... What did you say?" pointing to another member of the group.

Laughing, Dr. Rydell says, "You want Lou to tell you who you are?" Frustrated and tapping his foot, Dave tries one more time, "No, I just, uh, I'm a nice easygoing man. I might be a little bit indecisive at times, um...."

Still not satisfied, Dr. Rydell pushes again, "Dave, you're describing your personality. I want to know...who you are." Lunging forward in his chair, in an exasperated outburst, Dave says, "I don't know what the [heck] you want me to say!" With the room shifting in their chairs, Dave calms down, "I mean, I'm sorry. I just, I want to answer your question. Just not, not doing it right, I guess."

Over a hushed room, Dr. Rydell responds, "I think we're getting the picture...Dave."

Many of us feel like Dave. The world is asking, "Who are you?" And we're thinking, "I don't know what the heck you want me to say!" We simply don't have a clear answer. We think that who we are is about what we do or what we enjoy, but it's not. Your purpose embodies who you are, and your Natural Advantage is the foundation.

Your Natural Advantage is the role you tend to play in life and work.

It supports every other element of your Purpose Factor. It informs what skills you should acquire and develop through study or work experience. It supports your Pull-Passion as it starts to reveal the problem in the world that you want to solve. Your Natural Advantage helps you use your Origin Story to help others overcome what you overcame. Most importantly, it begins to give you clarity on who you are and what you're supposed to do next.

Unlocking the Role You Play

The idea of determining what you're good at and the role you play can feel overwhelming. You think, "I do a lot and I'm good at multiple things. I can't just pick one." Or perhaps you think, "I'm not good at a lot of things. I can't even think of one." But the truth is, while you play many roles, you tend to play one of those roles the best. The key to unlocking the remaining elements of your Purpose Factor is to identify which role you best play.

As the phrase suggests, your Natural Advantage comes naturally. You don't have to think about it. To others, it's a task, but to you, it's a breeze. That is why recognizing your Natural Advantage is often challenging. Because your Natural Advantage is second nature to you, it doesn't seem profound, exciting, or even useful. And because it isn't exciting, you often ignore it and try to play a different role. But by looking for excitement in the new and different, you end up avoiding what you had all along.

For example, you may start projects easily. You can start a new workout program, design a detailed strategy for paying off debt, or launch a project with little startup anxiety. You can do it without thinking. To you, starting is easy. To others, starting is terrifying. Or maybe you're naturally inquisitive. You wonder why things are done a certain way. You ask questions about processes, ingredients, and people. To you, asking questions is common sense. To others, asking questions doesn't make any sense. To you, your Natural Advantage doesn't seem like a big deal. To others, it's a very big deal, so don't ignore it.

Five Types of Natural Advantages

There are five types of Natural Advantages—the Builder, the Truth Teller, the Teacher, the Overseer, and the Recruiter. You

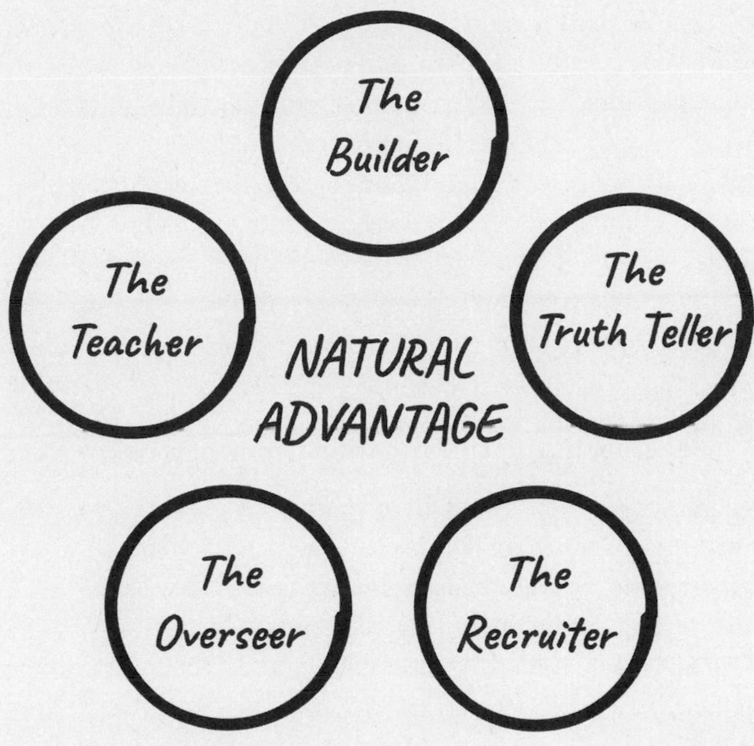

may have the characteristics of more than one Natural Advantage, but you only have one guiding Natural Advantage. And that *one* is the role that must be nurtured. It's the one you need to focus on growing the most. It should guide your career choices, life decisions, and areas of study and development.

As we've said, the quest for purpose is not about finding your "why," but determining who you are and who you can help. Your Natural Advantage helps you begin to answer the question "Who am I?" By identifying which of the five Natural Advantages you have, you will be able to discover the remaining elements of your Purpose Factor.

The Builder loves to start things. Whether that is launching new products at the company, new projects around the house, or coming up with new strategies to get more done, the Builder will make it happen. The Builder loves strategy. They enjoy bringing clarity to chaos, providing direction, and coming up with a plan. The Builder is drawn to job opportunities where they can strategize without oversight. They tend to take the lead in relationships and are driven to succeed.

The Truth Teller needs to know what is happening. They ask questions, pry further, and dig deeper to understand the truth. Truth Tellers are bold, outspoken, and are not afraid to have their voice be heard. They seem to predict the future as if they have a sixth sense. They are intuitive and have a passion for getting to the bottom of a complex issue. The Truth Teller is drawn to opportunities that let them dig into an issue, investigate what is unclear, and inform others of problems, injustice, or corruption.

The Teacher helps others understand. They are patient, enjoy coaching others, and love sharing their knowledge. They may teach by speaking, but they may also prefer to write down their insight. They are always learning and always sharing what they learn. The Teacher is drawn to career opportunities where they can help others understand. They are the interpreters of information who share their knowledge with the world.

The Overseer makes sure that everything is taken care of. They are organized, detail-oriented, and attentive to the needs of others. The Overseer is reliable and enjoys being the person that you can depend on, no matter what. The Overseer takes whatever is given to them and improves it. They take the initiative—usually without asking—to solve a problem. The Overseer is drawn to jobs that allow them to take care of others and develop organizational structure.

The Recruiter will make you want what they have. The Recruiter is convincing because they are a true believer. The Recruiter becomes a fan of what they love and can't help but share that love with others. They are constantly talking about how great something or someone is and want to get others as excited as they are. The Recruiter is drawn to opportunities that allow them to bring others into their world. They make great sales people, fundraisers, and brand ambassadors.

Questions to Determine Your Top Natural Advantage

The depth of your questions determines your level of discovery. Great questions produce great answers, and great answers are specific. Three questions will determine which Natural Advantage is your number one.

QUESTION ONE: AS A KID, WHAT ROLE DID YOU PLAY IN YOUR FAMILY?

Because your Natural Advantage is something that you are born with, it pops up early in your life. Consider the type of child you were. Were you known as the one who jumped first without worrying about the consequences? Were you unfazed by risk or potential failure? Did you start businesses as a kid or invent new ways of doing things around the house? If so, you may be a Builder.

Did you ask questions? Did you wonder why people did certain things or why things were the way they were? Did you have a bold personality, unafraid to speak your mind? If so, you may be a Truth Teller.

Did you like teaching your siblings or friends new things? Did you ask lots of questions to find out how something worked? Did taking a complex issue and making it simple get you excited? If so, you may be a Teacher.

Were you a caring kid? Did it bother you when people or animals were hurt or needed help? Did you look for opportunities that showed how responsible you were? Were you interested in games that included everybody? If so, you may be an Overseer.

Were you the one who convinced other kids to do something? Did you get friends or siblings to see things the way you saw them? Were you excited about sharing your favorite toys, experiences, or thoughts with others? If so, you may be a Recruiter.

QUESTION TWO: WHAT WOULD YOU DO ALL DAY IF YOU DIDN'T NEED MONEY?

To gain even more clarity on your Natural Advantage, let's look at what you enjoy doing. As we discussed in previous chapters, you enjoy what you are good at, and you are good at what comes naturally to you. Your Natural Advantage is hidden in what you do every day.

Do you like starting new projects? Even if it means that you don't finish, does the opportunity to launch a new project excite you? Do you enjoy planning for the future, defining goals, and solving complex issues? If so, you may be a Builder.

Do you like getting to the bottom of things? Does it bother you when there is misinformation in the news? If given a chance, would you spend a day investigating something or advocating on behalf of an issue important to you? If so, you may be a Truth Teller.

Do you like helping people discover a better way of doing things? Does it bother you when people don't know how to do something or where to get the information they need? Do you get energy sharing new information or insight that you have with others? If so, you may be a Teacher.

Do you like being there for people? Do you feel energized by helping other people with projects? It could be a personal issue, a home repair, or giving insight on a problem at work. If so, you may be an Overseer.

Do you like inviting people to events that are important to you? Do you get excited when others share your excitement about a product or movement? If so, you may be a Recruiter.

QUESTION THREE: WHY WOULD YOUR FRIENDS COME TO YOU FOR ADVICE?

Your Natural Advantage is experienced by others around you. This final question helps solidify your core Natural Advantage. It gives you an outside perspective on your natural brilliance.

Do your friends come to you for strategic advice? Do they come to you if they need help thinking through a problem? Do they need an expert perspective? Do they see you as someone who thinks big picture without getting emotional? If so, you may be a Builder.

Do your friends come to you for your honest opinion? If there is an election, an issue at work, or a trend in society, do they want to know your opinion? Are there issues that you are known to speak out about? Do your friends know your strong convictions and most immovable beliefs? If so, you may be a Truth Teller.

Do your friends come to you for help learning something new? Do they see you as the one who is patient enough to coach them through? Are you the one who will show others how to do something—whether that is how to cook, how to install a car radio, or how to apply to college? If so, you may be a Teacher.

Do your friends come to you for support? Do they know that if they give something to you, you will make it better? Are you known as the organized one? If something goes wrong—they lose someone, their car breaks down, they need help—do they know they can rely on you? If so, you may be an Overseer.

Do your friends come to you when they need to be convinced of something? Do they recruit you to get more friends to join, or more people to support a cause? Do you always have new people in your life? Do your friends joke about how much you are outspoken about your love for a particular product? If so, you may be a Recruiter.

Based on the questions above, which Natural Advantage do you leverage most of the time? Again, you may have the characteristics of more than one, but you only have one primary Natural Advantage.

Using Your Natural Advantage

Your Natural Advantage is the foundation of your Purpose Factor. It is the role you play and the innate qualities you have. We all have a primary Natural Advantage. It can be used and grown. It can also be abused and ignored. The deeper you investigate your Natural Advantage, the more clarity you will have on how you use your entire Purpose Factor to help others.

The most successful business leaders, influencers, and parents start with what they have, their Natural Advantage, and grow it. They do not deny what they are naturally good at, but they embrace their Natural Advantage and use it to help others. You have greatness within you. The height of your impact will be determined by how well you use your Natural Advantage.

So what is your primary Natural Advantage? Are you the Builder, Truth Teller, Teacher, Overseer, or Recruiter?

My Primary Natural Advantage is:

____.

Want to go deeper on discovering even more of your Purpose Factor? Visit **purposefactorbook.com/journal** for a personalized Purpose Factor experience.

12

Your Acquired Skills

"To each there comes in their lifetime a special moment when they are figuratively tapped on the shoulder and offered the chance to do a very special thing, unique to them and fitted to their talents. What a tragedy if that moment finds them unprepared or unqualified for that which could have been their finest hour." ***—Sir Winston Churchill***

When we were young, conversations about skills were simple. Were you better at English or science? Did you like sports or reading? But as we grow up, answers to the question, "What am I good at?" get more practical. We pick college majors and jobs because of our skills. We're hired and promoted because of our skills. Our economy is all about skills.

The second element of your Purpose Factor is your Acquired Skills.

We all know what skills are. They're the ability to do something well. When fully developed, skills become expertise. They define your value in the marketplace and help you take care of yourself and your family. But your skills are not only about getting jobs and taking care of yourself and your own. They are tools for you to use your Purpose Factor.

If your Purpose Factor is what you have to help others, your Acquired Skills are a big part of what you have. To live a good life, you must identify your Acquired Skills. To live a fulfilled life, you must grow your Acquired Skills. And to live a purposeful life, you must use those skills to help others.

That's because fulfillment requires personal growth, and growth is all about who you're becoming. It's not about your past successes or failures. Growth is not about what you've already done. What you've done is in the past, and the past is over. In essence, identifying your Acquired Skills is about answering the question, "Who am I becoming to help others more?"

As humans, we're designed to get better. One generation gave us electricity; another provided us with the internet. One generation put a man on the moon; another commercialized space travel. In order to move forward, we must grow.

Discovering your Natural Advantage is about identifying the role you were born to play. Identifying your Acquired Skills is about unlocking the secret to mobilizing your purpose. Your Acquired Skills are the abilities developed through school, training, and experience. Your skill could be throwing a football, baking cakes, defending criminals, or teaching kindergarten.

No matter what it is, identifying your number one Acquired Skill is essential to using your Purpose Factor to help others today, tomorrow, and in the future.

Becoming the G.O.A.T.

Being the G.O.A.T. or "Greatest of all time" is the ultimate compliment. It signifies that you have become the best in your field. You have achieved the top spot. You are number one. Many of us want to be great. But to be great, you must identify and grow your Acquired Skills.

The most successful people in the world know their Acquired Skills and grow their Acquired Skills. They don't leave it to luck to become the best in the world. They put in the work to get good at their craft. Just being "okay" is not okay. They know their ability exists for a reason. And one thing is for sure: they never stop growing. The most successful among us are constantly asking, "Who do I need to become to help more people?"

Top achievers identify their top Acquired Skill and go full tilt. They become the best, even in the face of uncertainty and adversity. They're not interested in being the best at everything; life's too short for that. They're interested in becoming the best at one thing.

Billionaire Warren Buffett started acquiring investing skills early. He made his first stock purchase at age eleven. While he earned a bachelor's in business administration and a master's in economics, he never stopped growing. He continued to build his Acquired Skills through experience, failed investments, and challenging business partnerships. He once told a Columbia Business School class that he reads as many as five hundred pages per day. Warren never lost focus. In early 2019, his Acquired Skills in investing made him the third-richest person in the world at $82.5 billion.

Oprah Winfrey was told that moving to Chicago to take over a daytime talk show was foolish. She did it anyway. To improve her craft, she would interview her audience after every show. Oprah knew that she wouldn't become the best unless she was willing to ask for real feedback. Oprah became an expert interviewer not by asking questions, but by listening. She listened to guests and audience members alike. Oprah leveraged her Acquired Skills to become a motivational icon and household name.

Having Acquired Skills in bodybuilding and winning Mr. Olympia seven times, Arnold Schwarzenegger wanted to become the highest-paid actor in the world. Hollywood agents said he was too big, too foreign, and too strange for television. But Arnold focused on who he was becoming. He acquired new skills in acting, honed his accent, and found a mentor in comedy great Lucille Ball.

Robert Kiyosaki, author of the number one personal finance book of all time *Rich Dad Poor Dad*, was told to go back to school and get a master's in business administration before starting a business. He ignored that advice and built his Acquired Skills in real estate and wealth creation on his own time. Now he teaches international audiences how to do the same.

The best in the world zero in on their top Acquired Skills. Then, they grow them. It takes more than an idea and hard work to become successful. Ideas without action are worthless, and hard work without direction is a hamster wheel. Titans develop their Acquired Skills on purpose and for a purpose. You will not discover the fullness of your Purpose Factor, help others, or experience maximum fulfillment if you don't identify and grow your Acquired Skills.

All for the Money

In August of 2019, a Reddit user known by the handle "Delicious-Garfield" posted a question:

> *My career counselor asked me this question: "If money was not a factor, what would you do with your life?" I really struggled to find the answer. What answer would you guys have given? Aren't we all in it for the money and prestige?*

Almost instantly, the responses flooded in. The question had hit a nerve. In one comment thread, users argued whether or not you can enjoy something without earning money. In another thread, there was discussion about what they would study and where they would travel if money wasn't an issue. Some responses were bitter while others were optimistic. But all the answers had one thing in common: their response was based on their belief about work.

What you believe about what you do matters.

If we believe work is bad, then we'll see it as a means to an end. If work is bad, it's less about helping others with what we have and more about getting by. On the other hand, if we believe work is good, we'll help others and experience personal fulfillment.

When you acquire skills and grow them to help others, you're more likely to enjoy your work. High achievers live for transformations, not transactions. And the more they focus on transformation, the more transactions they get.

In 2018, we were speaking at a large nursing conference. We asked the audience a simple question: "Why did you choose your field?" It's a question we've asked hundreds of times to audiences across the country. The answers were as we expected. We heard, "I wanted to help people," "My mom was a nurse," and, "It seemed like a fulfilling career choice."

But then, from a woman in the front, we got an extra dose of honesty. She said, "I was between becoming a nurse or a bookkeeper. Nursing paid better." This woman had chosen her entire life's path based on earning potential alone. That choice likely influenced who she would marry, where she would move, and where her kids would go to school.

Money alone will not fulfill you. Fulfillment comes from choosing a career that connects your purpose to what you do every day. When you do, it feels less like work and more like purpose.

Five Rules for Identifying Your Acquired Skills

Brian briefly worked at a men's suit shop in college. He took tailoring measurements, stocked shelves, and straightened neckties. After a few months on the job, he noticed a pattern. During their fittings, men would ask, "I'm going to be losing a few pounds in the next six months, can you take the measurements slightly smaller?"

It happened so often that Brian's boss taught all the salesmen to say in response, "That's great, but I can only fit you as you are."

Many of us want to utilize the skills we don't have. We inflate resumes with languages we don't speak well, proficiencies we no longer have, and abilities that aren't relevant. Like Brian's suit shop manager, we must measure our skills "as they are."

In taking that measurement, there are five rules for identifying your top Acquired Skill—the one you want to focus on growing. You may have many skills that you have developed. You may have gotten those abilities through different experiences, jobs, and industries. To effectively use your skills to help people, you must identify your top Acquired Skill.

Rule #1—You Have Received Training in Your Acquired Skill

The greatest Acquired Skills are developed intentionally.

Ben and Jerry took a five-dollar course on ice cream making and turned it into a creamy empire. Steve Jobs took college courses in calligraphy and created the most beautiful technology available. In the 1980s, Roxanne Quimby learned how to make beeswax lip balm from a nineteenth-century cookbook, and Burt's Bees took off.

Acquired Skills are acquired through a process, whether simple or complicated, free or for a fee. You could have been trained through schooling, certifications, or mentoring. Or you could have been trained through life experience, prison, or personal study. How you acquired your skills is not important. How you grow and use them is everything.

If you believe you have a skill but have not worked to improve it, it's not an Acquired Skill. It may be an interest or a hobby, but not an Acquired Skill. **Until you take it seriously, you can't expect the world to take you seriously.**

Rule #2—You Can Use Your Acquired Skill to Offer Value

When Howard Schultz took over Starbucks, there were other coffee chains in America. When Chick-fil-A came on the scene, it had to compete with megabrands like McDonald's. Michael Jordan wasn't the first great basketball player, and Leonardo DiCaprio wasn't the first Hollywood star. Yet, these brands and people became the best by providing extreme value to others.

Starbucks sought to create the best, most consistent coffee and wanted a location on every corner. Chick-fil-A wanted to create the best chicken sandwich and the best customer service. Your Acquired Skills are the value you offer to the world around you. They're also the skills that others will reward you for.

In the marketplace of ideas, your value is determined by how much others want the Acquired Skills that you have. Your value could be creating great art, excellent pasta, or a process that reinvents how coffee is made. Remember, there's always room at the top when you focus on providing extreme value to the people you're meant to help.

Rule #3—Your Acquired Skill Is Something You Want to Improve

The late Bruce Lee said, "We are told that talent creates opportunity, yet it is desire that creates talent." The strongest Acquired Skills are those that are intentionally developed. They start with what Bruce Lee calls "desire." One secret to identifying your top Acquired Skill is to determine which skill you want to improve the most. The desire to improve (and grow) is the secret to endurance. The more you are willing to grow and adapt, the more you will succeed. And you will only succeed when you are willing to sacrifice.

When you see others who have given up on their dreams, it's not because they reached their max potential; it's because they stopped sacrificing to achieve their max potential. As John Maxwell said, "You have to give up to go up."

French novelist Honoré de Balzac said, "There is no such thing as a great talent without great willpower." You must be willing to improve your top Acquired Skill or else it will atrophy and become worthless.

Rule #4—Your Acquired Skill Is about Helping Other People

Henry Ford said, "The man who will use his skill and constructive imagination to see how much he can give for a dollar, instead of how little he can give for a dollar, is bound to succeed."

As we've said before, purpose isn't passion alone, and passion is never your starting point. You may not be passionate about your Acquired Skills yet, but you will become passionate about them as you grow them. How? Because as you become more proficient in your skills, you will be able to help more people. As you grow, your passion grows. As you grow, your value grows. As you grow, others grow. As you grow, your fulfillment grows.

The number one thing that will give meaning to your work is that your work transforms others. In other words, who are you helping with your top Acquired Skill?

Rule #5—Your Acquired Skill Aligns with Your Desired Lifestyle

Investor Mark Cuban said, “If you really want to know where your destiny lies, look at where you apply your time. Time is the most valuable asset you don’t own. You may or may not realize it, but how you use or don’t use your time is going to be the best indication of where your future is going to take you.”

How you spend your time is how you’ll spend your life. Many people pursue skills that aren’t aligned with how they want to spend their life. They want to be a nurse but don’t like blood. They want to be an entrepreneur but don’t like risk. You will not enjoy your work, and you won’t help others, if your lifestyle isn’t aligned with your Acquired Skills.

Determine whether your Acquired Skills currently align with your desired lifestyle and current values. If they do, continue to grow in them. If not, it may be time to readjust where you develop your brilliance.

Five Types of Acquired Skills

Acquired Skills are more than what you do for work. Acquired Skills are tools that you have acquired throughout your life. You may not be in a job that reflects your Acquired Skills. Perhaps you aren’t in a traditional job; you are retired, raising children,

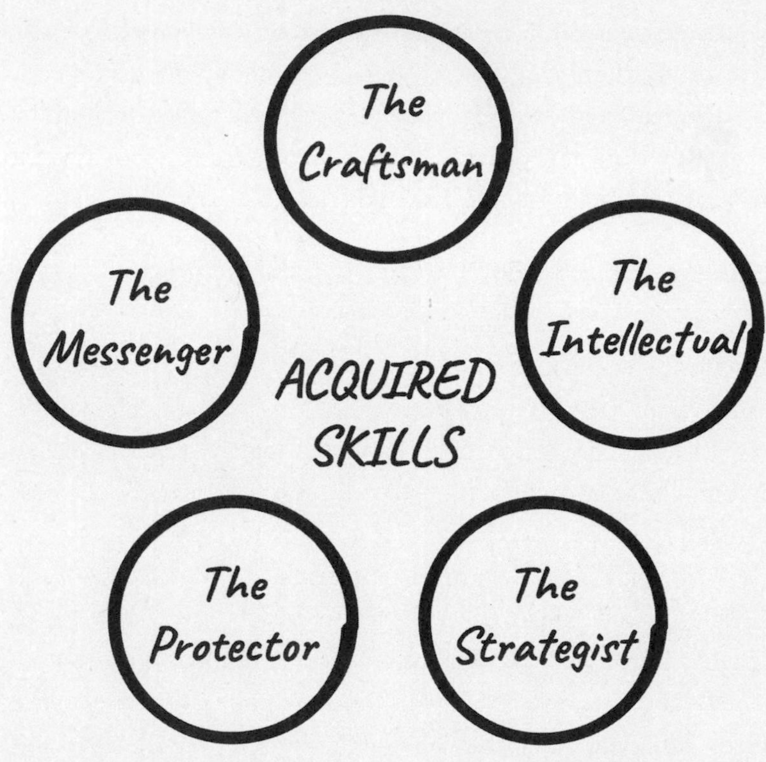

or out of the workforce. Employment status does not determine your ability to use your Acquired Skills to help others.

Like Natural Advantage, there are five different types of Acquired Skills. Not one skill is more valuable or more useful to have. Each type of Acquired Skill is equally important to the world.

The Craftsman does things with their hands or body. This could be an athlete, an HVAC technician, or a hairstylist. Their job is a physical one as they build, repair, and create with their body. They prefer working on a project that has a real and tangible result. They work well with others but work as if it all relies on them.

The Intellectual thinks, writes, and creates. This could be a professor, an inventor, an artist, a researcher, or a doctor. They do well with abstract notions and are fine working on a project that does not have a clearly defined end. They enjoy collaboration and feel inspired and motivated when working alongside others.

The Messenger communicates, translates, and transmits information for others. This could be a journalist, a videographer, a television personality, or a copyeditor. They like high-stakes projects and working under a deadline—even if that deadline is imposed by themselves. They see others as partners in collaboration and distribution but are quick to get frustrated if others do not share their vision.

The Protector takes care of people or things. This could be a lawyer, human resources professional, or stay-at-home parent. They analyze risk and organize things. They work well managing multiple and often competing priorities. Protectors make decision-making simpler for others. They protect the status quo and put others above themselves.

The Strategist comes up with the plan others follow. This could be an investor, a coach, an executive, or an attorney. They enjoy reverse engineering problems and creating a clear and linear plan. They are very data-driven, but can also work with ideas that aren't fully formed. Strategists are tasked with making difficult decisions.

Questions to Identify Your Top Acquired Skill

The following questions are designed to take you by the hand and help you discover your top Acquired Skill. Remember, you may have many skills that you have acquired and developed throughout your lifetime. To best harness the power of your Purpose Factor, you must identify your number one skill.

QUESTION ONE: WHAT DO YOU SPEND MOST OF YOUR DAY DOING?

Because your top Acquired Skill is something that you have developed an expertise in, it is easiest to look at what you spend most of your time doing. Consider what type of activities you do all day.

Do you tend to move physically throughout the day? Are you on your feet, building, serving, or performing? Do you find yourself more physically tired than mentally tired at the end of the day? If so, you may be a Craftsman.

Do you spend most of your time considering abstract ideas? Do you analyze complicated issues? Do you like getting alone with your thoughts to solve a problem or consider the possibilities? If so, you may be an Intellectual.

Do you spend most of your day communicating in some way? It could be writing blogs, books, producing news segments, or speaking to audiences. If so, you may be a Messenger.

Do you spend your days organizing chaos? Are you brought in to make sure that things are running smoothly? It could be managing people, reorganizing a closet, or auditing the annual budget. If so, you may be a Protector.

Do you spend your days making big decisions? Are you the one who is given the final word, asked to consider multiple options, and gives direction for the future? If so, you may be a Strategist.

QUESTION TWO: WHAT WOULD SOMEONE PAY YOU MONEY TO DO FOR THEM?

Your Acquired Skills must provide value to you and to others. Review the following section and consider where you bring the most value to others.

Do people pay you for what you do physically? Do they want you to build something for them, perform something for them, or play a sport badly enough that they are willing to pay for it? And not just willing—but they are actually paying for it (ability and action are very different!). If so, you may be a Craftsman.

Do people pay you for your thoughts and opinions? Do they value your unique perspective and how you deliver it so much that you are compensated for sharing it? If so, you may be an Intellectual.

Do people pay you for your ability to communicate? Do they invest in your books, your movies, your songs, or your performance on television? If so, you may be a Messenger.

Do people pay you for your ability to handle the details? Do they value your ability to manage people, finances, schedules, or agendas? If so, you may be a Protector.

Do people pay you because of your leadership? Do you receive compensation for your specific skill in strategy and foresight? This could be as an executive, an investor, a board member, or a consultant. If so, you may be a Strategist.

QUESTION THREE: WHAT ACCOMPLISHMENT ARE YOU MOST PROUD OF?

Your Acquired Skills are beyond just what you do. They also encompass what you enjoy doing. Review the following section and identify where you get the most fulfillment helping others.

Consider your biggest accomplishment, outside of becoming a parent. Think about a time when you created something, delivered something, or worked on something. It could be a major deal, a presentation, or even a school project.

What type of work were you doing?

Think specifically about that moment. What about that work energized you?

On that day, who were you serving?

As you consider the questions, which top Acquired Skill can you use to help others by providing the most value? As with your Natural Advantage, you may have multiple skills but only one top Acquired Skill.

What If I Don't Like My Acquired Skills?

If you're younger, your Acquired Skills may not be developed. Perhaps you have some Acquired Skills but still need to grow in them. If you're older, you may have grown tired of the work you do and would like to acquire new skills. In either situation, that's okay.

If you're younger, consider your number one Natural Advantage, the role you were born to play. For example, if you play the role of the Builder, you may want to consider acquiring skills as a Messenger or Strategist. If you are a Truth Teller, you might want to consider acquiring skills as an Intellectual or Strategist. In the beginning, your Natural Advantage helps inform your Acquired Skills.

If you have developed skills in an area you don't enjoy, know this: not one moment of your life has been a waste. Every second you've experienced has equipped you with the ability to help others. Losses, failures, traumas, betrayals, and rejections tend to make us feel that we've wasted time. If you believe everything can be used for a reason, you don't curse the days on the job that you hate.

One thing is true: whether you're young or old, it's neither too early nor too late to discover the elements of your Purpose

Factor and help others. Youth equals energy and age equals wisdom. **And no matter your age, oxygen equals purpose.** If you're still breathing, you're here to help others and leave a legacy of transformation.

What is your top Acquired Skill? Are you the Craftsman, Intellectual, Messenger, Protector, or the Strategist?

My Top Acquired Skill is:

____.

13

Your Pull-Passion

There is an old Korean folktale called "The Story Bag." In the tale, a young boy is passionate about great stories. He loves stories so much that he asks every person he meets to tell him a different one. Each time, he listens and puts the stories in a bag on his belt. He keeps them there for his pleasure and never shares them. After years of collecting stories, the bag is stuffed to the brim.

Eventually, the young boy grows up, but the stories in the bag grow angry. They are tired of being crammed together and untold. As the boy is preparing to get married, the stories decide they will kill him on his wedding night. But a faithful servant overhears the stories' plan and rescues the boy from the wrath of the untold stories.

The moral of the story: stories are for sharing, not for stealing. This short Korean story offers us a warning. If we use our passion for us alone, bad things happen. If we make our passion about others and their transformation, powerful things happen.

Our lives changed the day we realized that our passion (and purpose) wasn't about us. If we were going to stay motivated, our passion had to be bigger than us. It had to pull us forward and drive us to help others. That was the day we discovered Pull-Passion, the third element of your Purpose Factor.

Your Pull-Passion is the problem in the world that you're made to solve.

Now that you know your Natural Advantage and your top Acquired Skill, you're ready to discover and define your Pull-Passion.

Good Passion, Bad Passion

Much has been written about passion, and most of it doesn't make sense. Jon Bon Jovi said, "Nothing is as important as passion. No matter what you want to do with your life, be passionate."

But Sir Philip Sidney, a prominent poet of the Elizabethan era, explained, "He whom passion rules, is bent to meet his death."

Motivational titan Tony Robbins stated, "Passion is the genesis of genius."

And French philosopher François de La Rochefoucauld wrote, "Passion makes idiots of the cleverest men, and makes the biggest idiots clever."

So is passion the road to destruction or the path to prominence? Depending on how you look at it, it's both.

The ancient Greeks had a word for passion. Their word was "pathos," which had both good and bad uses. Pathos was used to express emotion and empathy but also suffering and misfortune. The truth is, passion can produce clarity or confusion, direction or distraction, joy or pain.

That's because, by definition, passion is a "barely controllable emotion." On the one hand, you could have a barely controllable emotion to end child hunger, which could drive you to raise money and run food drives—a good passion. On the other hand, you could have a barely controllable emotion for eating ice cream, which could drive you to gain weight and become sick—a bad passion.

The difference between good passion and bad passion is why discovering your Pull-Passion is so important. Passion alone is a barely controllable emotion, but your Pull-Passion is the problem in the world you're meant to solve. Passion is all about you and your feelings. Pull-Passion is all about others and how you can help them. Passion is selfish. Pull-Passion is selfless. Passion asks, "What do I like?" Pull-Passion asks, "How can I help?" Passion produces feelings that flare up and fade. Pull-Passion creates a steady stream of energy through good times and bad.

So how do you avoid the path of destruction and accurately identify your Pull-Passion? You put it in the context of your Purpose Factor.

An ancient proverb states, "Our passions are winds that propel our vessel. Our reason is the pilot that steers her. Without winds, the vessel would not move, and without a pilot, she would be lost." Benjamin Franklin agreed. He suggested, "If passion drives you, let reason hold the reins."

Your Pull-Passion may drive you forward, but your Purpose Factor is the reins.

When Passion Pulls You

Imagine that we handed you and a friend a rope. We gave one end of the rope to your friend and the other to you. Then we told you to stand behind your friend. Finally, we told you to push your friend six feet forward, using only the rope. You'd think we're crazy. That's because it's impossible to push someone using a limp rope.

However, if we asked you to stand in front of your friend and pull them six feet forward using only the rope, you would have no problem. Pulling is easier than pushing. The same is true in life. It's easier to be pulled by purpose than to be pushed around by circumstances. You know the difference. It's the difference between snoozing your alarm because you dread work and bouncing out of bed because you're excited for the day. The only way to create that kind of pull in your life is to identify your Pull-Passion.

The power of pull is obvious in the lives of top performers. When Jim Carrey started acting, he wrote himself a check for $10 million for "acting services rendered" to pull him to become one of the best actors in the world.

At age thirteen, surfer Bethany Hamilton lost her arm to a shark bite. Despite the attack, she was back on her surfboard a month later. She was pulled by the opportunity to teach others to overcome their setbacks.

By starting with your Natural Advantage, you discover the role you were born to play. By identifying your Acquired Skill, you discover the tools you have to help others. Now, you will find your Pull-Passion—the problem, need, injustice, desire, or hurt in the world you're meant to solve. To find your Pull-Passion is to find your source of energy.

Five Types of Pull-Passions

As with the other elements of The Purpose Factor, there are five types of Pull-Passions. Each Pull-Passion represents the problem in the world you want to solve. You may have more than one Pull-Passion. Focus on the most compelling problem that pulls you.

The Problem Solver goes after big issues. They see global issues as problems that need to be solved immediately. To them, the problem seems to be everywhere; they can get frustrated when others don't see the problem as they do. This could include dismantling corrupt governments, improving traffic patterns, or helping people find purpose. The Problem Solver is passionate

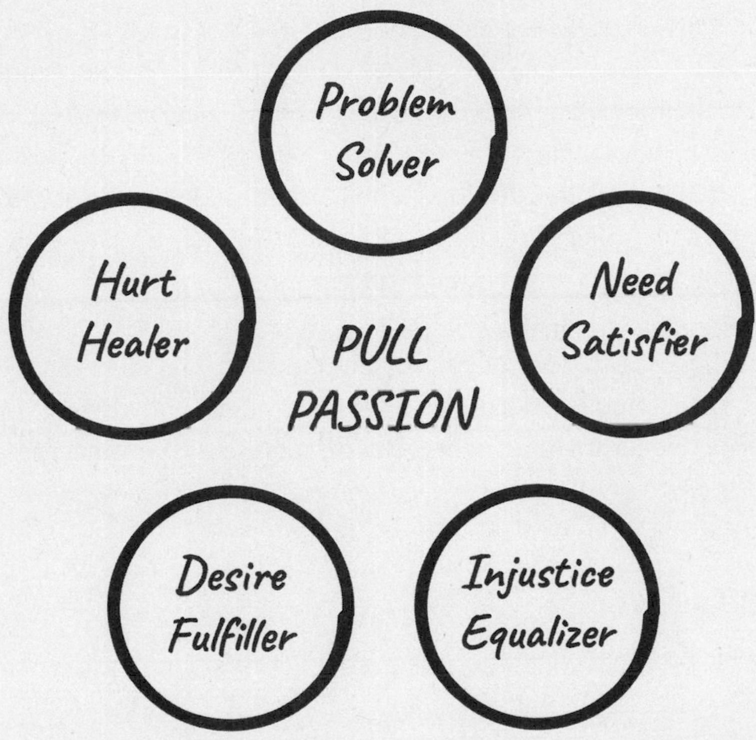

about finding solutions to issues that others think are too big or too complicated to address.

The Need Satisfier is excited about opportunities to serve individuals' needs. Unlike the Problem Solver who looks at the big picture, the Need Satisfier is focused on helping a specific group of people—or even a single person. They identify areas that people are lacking, typically when it comes to surviving or living well. It could be access to clean water in your city, removing barriers to entry for female business owners, or creating an app that helps students manage their finances. The Need Satisfier is passionate about service.

The Hurt Healer fixes emotional and physical hurt. This could be eradicating a disease, helping people recover from addiction, or taking in rescue dogs. The Hurt Healer is passionate about making things better for those who need to be made whole.

The Desire Fulfiller sees a hole in the market and seeks to fill it with their skills or interests. It could be filling the desire for people to laugh, the desire for adventure, or the desire to have faster internet speeds. The Desire Fulfiller seeks to improve the quality of life or level of enjoyment for others.

The Injustice Equalizer is drawn to issues of equality. It could be equal voting rights, diverse representation on corporate boards, or restoring abused women. The Injustice Equalizer is passionate about making wrong things right.

Determining Your Pull-Passion

Your Pull-Passion will inspire you to take action. It will cause you to get out of your comfort zone, help others, and experience fulfillment. It will challenge you to grow in your Natural Advantage and Acquired Skills. Your Pull-Passion will help you make sense of your next move. To determine your Pull-Passion, ask yourself the following two questions.

QUESTION ONE: WHAT PROBLEM IN THE WORLD UPSETS YOU THE MOST?

Typically, your Pull-Passion will be something in the world that breaks your heart or frustrates you. What do you talk about the most or complain about the most? What problem, need, injustice, desire, or hurt in the world gets your attention? Does it fire you up in the morning or keep you up at night? Consider the following:

Are you upset when others don't seem concerned about big issues? Are you most upset about societal issues that others shrug off? Are you noticing the problem throughout your day? If so, you may be a Problem Solver.

Are you most upset when people's basic needs are mishandled? Are you drawn to solving problems for others that they can't solve for themselves? If so, you may be a Need Satisfier.

Are you most upset when you see others are hurting physically or emotionally? Do you get frustrated when the safety of people or animals is in jeopardy? If so, you may be a Hurt Healer.

Are you upset when others are doing something that you could be doing? Do you get annoyed or frustrated with how others are doing it (whatever "it" is)? Are you convinced you would do it better? If so, you may be a Desire Fulfiller.

Are you most upset when there is injustice? Do you stay up at night thinking about inequality and how there must be a way to make it right? If so, you may be an Injustice Equalizer.

QUESTION TWO: ARE YOU WILLING TO SACRIFICE FOR IT?

As you think about what type of Pull-Passion you have, a few things may come to mind. The best way to test your Pull-Passion is to consider your willingness to sacrifice. Sometimes, young entrepreneurs will ask us to mentor them. And though it's one of our favorite things to do, we can't mentor everyone. Before we agree to mentor someone, we test their level of commitment.

Once they've shared their goals with us, we ask them to sacrifice something keeping them from their goals, like television, time with friends, or coffee shop trips.

The ones who sacrifice have identified their Pull-Passion and are ready to take action. So we mentor them. The ones who don't want to sacrifice anything are not ready to take action. Why do we do this? Living out your Purpose Factor by helping others will require sacrifice. Experiencing the best requires giving up the second best. Consider the following:

Are you willing to sacrifice to make sure a big issue is solved? Are you giving up sleep, finances, and relationships to solve that problem? If so, you may be a Problem Solver.

Are you willing to sacrifice to meet the needs of others? Are you willing to lose money or your reputation so that others are taken care of? If so, you may be a Need Satisfier.

Are you willing to give up so others are made whole? Do you lose sleep when you find out someone has a disease? Does it break your heart when you know someone is in pain or suffering? If so, you may be a Hurt Healer.

Are you willing to sacrifice so that the desire of others can be fulfilled? Do you give up reasonable opportunities because you would rather meet the desires and interests of a group of people? If so, you may be a Desire Fulfiller.

Are you sacrificing to make things that are wrong right? Have you given up jobs, opportunities, and relationships to make sure the right thing is done? If so, you may be an Injustice Equalizer.

There All Along?

Sometimes we discover that we've been overlooking our Pull-Passion.

Russian author Leo Tolstoy wrote one of his famous short stories essentially about Pull-Passion. The story is about a man named Martin who fixes boots in his basement shop. After both his wife and children die, he wonders whether life is worth living.

Then Martin meets a man who is on his way to a monastery. The man tells him to stop living for himself and start living for

God. Martin listens. Late one night, Martin is sitting in his shop and hears God call him by name, "Martin, Martin! Look out into the street tomorrow, for I shall come."

The next day, Martin sits by the window looking for God in the faces passing by. While waiting, he takes in an old soldier and serves him tea. He helps a woman and her baby escape the cold and protects a boy who is being beaten. At the end of the day, Martin turns in for the night and remembers that he didn't see God that day. But then, God reminds Martin that he did see him. God was in the soldier, the woman, and the boy.

Often our Pull-Passion was there all along. We simply didn't notice it or have the words to describe it. It was something that was pulling us, but we never allowed ourselves to pursue it. Nonetheless, your Pull-Passion is your greatest opportunity to help others with what you have. It's the problem, need, injustice, desire, or hurt in the world that you're drawn to. It's the thing the both breaks your heart and drives you into the future.

Your Pull-Passion is the motivational engine of your Purpose Factor. It empowers you to make wise decisions. It helps you choose the right jobs to take, causes to support, and projects to work on. Perhaps you never had clarity on your passion. Now you do.

So what is your primary Pull-Passion? Are you the Problem Solver, Need Satisfier, Hurt Healer, Desire Fulfiller, or the Injustice Equalizer?

My Pull-Passion is:

____.

You act on what you believe. Change your beliefs, change your actions.

14

Your Origin Story

It was sometime before the age of ten when Brian was playing upstairs in the home of a childhood friend. A boy, a few years older than Brian, grabbed him and pulled him in the closet to "play a game." It was there that Brian was molested.

It happened in a moment. Despite having two incredible parents, there was nothing that anyone could have done to stop it.

Like many who have had unwanted sexual encounters, Brian struggled with guilt, shame, and anger. Then something happened. When he connected his Origin Story with that childhood moment, he realized that he wasn't a victim. He was a victor. He didn't have to be bitter anymore. He could be grateful. He didn't have to feel ashamed anymore. He could leverage the Origin Story of his Purpose Factor to help others.

That is Brian's Origin Story. Gabrielle's is different.

Gabrielle's entire family were loving and supportive, but one of the family members she looked up to most struggled with alcohol. When they were drinking, they were physically there, but mentally gone. One day, Gabrielle overheard something about wishing there was a boy in the family.

If she were a boy, would they not drink? If she did better in sports, would they be happier? Gabrielle would spend the next decade trying to prove to her family (and herself) that she was worthy of love.

Like Brian, when Gabrielle realized that moment was her Origin Story, it gave her extreme clarity. Her frustration turned into gratefulness. She realized that her family member's struggles were theirs to deal with, not hers. Gabrielle could now take responsibility for how she allowed those words to influence her choices.

Origin Stories are written when things happen to you or when things happen because of you. No matter how they form, Origin Stories are the events or series of events that most shape the way you see the world.

When others shape our Origin Story, they often don't realize the impact of their actions. In Brian's case, that boy had no idea his actions would cause so much grief or hardship. Gabrielle's family member likely didn't realize that their words would influence her sense of self-worth.

The final and most powerful element of your Purpose Factor is your Origin Story.

Your Natural Advantage defined your starting point. Your Acquired Skills defined your value in the marketplace. Your Pull-Passion gave you motivation. And your Origin Story is about to shape your perspective.

The Epic Journey You Are On

"A long time ago in a galaxy far, far away...."

"Call me Ishmael."

"It was the best of times, it was the worst of times...."

These are the opening lines of well-known epic stories. Although *Star Wars*, *Moby Dick*, and *A Tale of Two Cities* have very different storylines, they have something in common. They tell the tale of overcoming.

When George Lucas started writing the script for *Star Wars* in 1973, it didn't come easily. But two years later, he picked up a book called *The Hero with a Thousand Faces* by Joseph Campbell.

In it, Joseph breaks down what's now called the "hero's journey," and it has been used as the overarching story structure of nearly every adventure movie.

Here's how the hero's journey goes.

The hero is stuck in a stagnant, predictable world, and longs for something more. That's when they meet a mentor who offers them a challenge. Though the hero rejects the challenge at first because it seems too hard, they eventually give in. It is then that the hero enters an unknown world, facing struggles, self-doubt, and setbacks. But ultimately, the hero returns to their world victorious. In other words, the hero's journey has three parts: departure from the known, adventure in overcoming a challenge, and return with newfound knowledge and experience.

As you discover your Purpose Factor, you're on your own hero's journey. You left the world of conformity and complacency because you weren't satisfied with the status quo. You longed for something more. So here you are, on this journey to discover who you are and who you can help.

You're overcoming struggles, self-doubt, and mental roadblocks. You're unpacking the four elements of your Purpose Factor and exactly how to use them. At the end of this journey, you'll return to your world—your job, your kids, and your responsibilities—with newfound clarity.

Part of your hero's journey is discovering your Origin Story.

Your Origin Story is the moment or series of moments that most shaped the way you see the world.

It's like when Spiderman got his superpowers after getting bitten by a radioactive spider. It's Franklin Delano Roosevelt overcoming depression after his polio diagnosis. It's Bilbo Baggins on his quest for the ring. It's Hellen Keller learning to communicate.

Out of all the elements of your Purpose Factor, your Origin Story sets you apart. It gives you superpowers as it's entirely unique to you. Your Origin Story is so essential that author Simon Sinek admits that your "why" is essentially your Origin Story.

No matter your Origin Story, you'll come to find that it's a gift to help others.

Growing up, the world wanted us to believe the opposite: "What happened to you is what happened to you. Deal with it." Things happen to us, not for us. We heard, "Don't get your hopes up, things probably won't work out," and, "It's probably not meant to be." Over time, despite being capable of incredible feats, we took on this victim mindset. **But victims never win, and those who blame others never overcome.**

Your Purpose Factor and its Origin Story are powerful because everything that happened to you really happened for you. The good, bad, and everything in between equipped you to help others and experience maximum personal fulfillment. When you own your Origin Story, you realize how much you can control your destiny.

We're All Overcoming Something

All great stories are overcomer stories. In movies like *The Hunger Games*, *Gladiator*, and *My Fair Lady*, the main characters are overcoming the odds and being transformed in the process. Football legend Lou Holtz said it best: "Show me someone who has done something worthwhile, and I'll show you someone who has overcome adversity."

We're all overcoming something. Perhaps you are overcoming feelings of rejection after a divorce. Maybe you're overcoming an addiction, failure, or loss that's shaken you to the core. Maybe your Origin Story is recovering from a car accident, experiencing physical abuse, or losing a loved one. Perhaps it's overcoming the feeling that your parents never thought you were good enough. Maybe you won the lottery, and it ended up destroying you. Your story may have happened to you or because of you. Whatever your Origin Story is, it isn't for you. It's been given to you to help others.

When Grace discovered her Origin Story, it shifted her perspective. When we met Grace, she was an event planner at a prominent nonprofit. Though she found herself regularly assisting top leaders and foreign dignitaries, she wanted more.

Grace attended a weekend retreat where folks work with us to discover their Purpose Factor and put together an execution plan. While there, we dove into Grace's Origin Story.

When we identified her Origin Story as a Rejection Overcomer, it was the final step in unpacking her Purpose Factor. It was like the four-digit code on a padlock had just lined up. She could see why she was attracted to jobs that allowed her to help others feel welcome. After that weekend, Grace's perspective changed. So did her life. She was called in to interview for a job at the White House. She applied to two graduate programs at Oxford. She was invited to go to Africa to help orphans and met with the head of leadership development for the African Union. By the time she told us this, she had accepted a job with the World Food Programme and had moved to Rome.

She later wrote us an email:

> *I wanted you to know just how grateful I am for the weekend that we all had together. I walked away with a paradigm shift that has affected the scale of my vision for the future, as well as my approach to a number of my relationships. In recent weeks,*

I have been progressing from a posture of waiting for permission to launch, and have been taking ownership for what I feel has been placed on my heart to do in the years ahead. I went from feeling like I was stalling and suspended to feeling like I have been launched into a whole new level professionally and personally!

Grace was able to take what happened to her and use it to help others find peace and comfort. She transformed her Origin Story into her permission to live out the other elements of her Purpose Factor. Grace's is just one of many stories we hear from folks who are reframing their Origin Stories and seeing incredible results.

Why We Don't Talk About Our Stories

As a society, we are obsessed with stories. Movies are long stories. Commercials are thirty-second stories. The news is a story. Your Facebook and Instagram feeds are stories. But most of the time, we hide our own stories because we don't want to be judged.

When we teach the Purpose Factor at companies, human resources often pulls us aside beforehand. They ask, "Is there anything we should know about the kinds of questions you're going to ask?" They're okay with us discussing employees' Natural Advantages, Acquired Skills, and even Pull-Passions. But when we get to Origin Story, they get nervous. And it's a shame.

Today, companies only use one element of an employee's Purpose Factor, their Acquired Skills. They don't ask questions about Natural Advantage so they have no idea about the role they will play in the company. They don't seem to care about Pull-Passion so they don't know what drives them to do good work. They certainly don't dive into Origin Story because they believe the lie that personal has nothing to do with professional. Imagine what our companies would look like if we had employees, managers, and executives driven by their Purpose Factor—the one thing that tells them, "You matter."

Companies aren't the only ones afraid of talking about Origin Stories. Most of us are. There are four reasons why:

1. Sharing doesn't feel appropriate. We assume that what has happened to us is too personal to share. We avoid sharing it with friends, colleagues, and those closest to us.
2. We're afraid of rejection. What would people think if they really knew? We fear that others will judge us, reject us, or treat us differently if we tell them what we have gone through.
3. We haven't processed our story. This is the most common reason why we don't share our Origin Stories. We push the hurt down, saying, "I'll deal with it later." We may even pretend it never happened. But what gets pushed down bubbles back up, often when we don't want it to.
4. We're ashamed. Sometimes we don't use our Origin Story to help others because we're ashamed of what we had to overcome. We've been fooled into thinking that what we have isn't a gift to help others or it can't be used for good.

Vulnerability is essential to knowing and living out your Purpose Factor. If you aren't honest with yourself, you won't be honest with others. If you don't know where you came from, you won't get clarity as to where you're going. If you don't discover who you are, you won't discover who you can help. **The truth is, we have to deal with our past to develop our future.**

Five Types of Origin Stories

Like the other elements of the Purpose Factor, there are five types of Origin Stories. Only you can determine what event most shaped the way you see the world. We have had someone who escaped an abusive relationship and had a tumor removed from their brain identify their Origin Story as their parents' divorce. Only you can identify that moment or series of moments that changed how you see yourself and how you see others. By effectively identifying your Origin Story, you will gain more clarity than you thought possible about who you are and how you live your life.

The Loss Overcomer has experienced a personal loss in their life. Typically, it is the death of a person very close to them, but it can also include the loss of a marriage or bankruptcy. Whatever it was, the event caused them to feel less than whole. Loss Overcomers can reflect on their life and notice that before this event, they were one way, and after this event, they were very different.

The Betrayal Overcomer knows what it means to be used. Perhaps they placed their trust in someone, and that person turned on them. Maybe the act of betrayal has cost them relationships, wealth, influence, or status. The moment, or series of moments, has been the most influential in shaping how they see the world.

The Failure Overcomer experienced a self-inflicted failure. It could be losing a business, getting kicked off of a team, or falling to addiction. This type of Origin Story is unique in that it is the only type that is caused by you. The others are a result of someone doing something to you. This makes it one of the most difficult to overcome, as it brings with it shame and self-doubt. It is also the most powerful when used to help others.

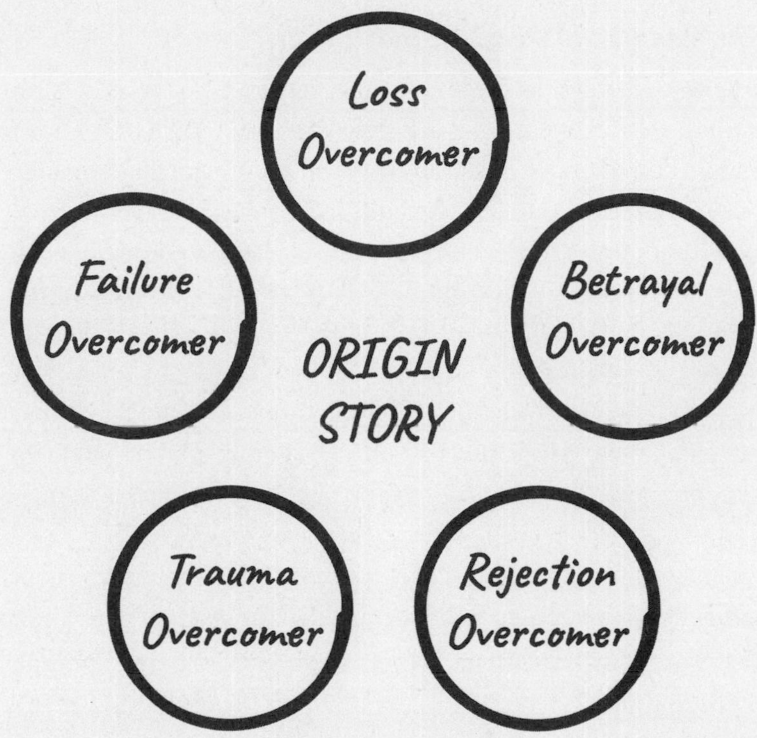

The Trauma Overcomer experienced a deeply impactful trauma. This trauma could be sexual assault, being abused by a parent, or losing the ability to hear. Typically the physical or emotional trauma is contained in a single event, but it can also occur over a series of years.

The Rejection Overcomer has been pushed away by people they care about. Rejection could be by a family member or lover. It could include denial for something they did, for who they are, or for who they aren't. They seek acceptance in relationships of all kinds, but can never seem to find the fulfillment they seek. They are afraid that if they show their true selves, they will not be accepted.

The Question to Discover Your Origin Story

Unlike the other elements of your Purpose Factor, you only have to answer one question to discover your Origin Story. It's a simple but powerful question. If you give an honest answer, get ready to experience a massive shift in your perspective.

QUESTION: EARLY IN LIFE, WHICH MOMENT OR SERIES OF MOMENTS MOST SHAPED THE WAY YOU SEE THE WORLD?

We all experience life-changing moments. For some, those moments are clearly defined. You can think back and label them without much reflection. For others, finding that moment or series of moments takes more time. If you can't identify a single moment, consider a situation that most shaped you. Maybe it was how you were raised. Then continue focusing in on a single moment that most characterizes that situation. It could be a fight that your parents got in or a day that you were left at school. The more specific you can be with the moment of your Origin Story, the more breakthrough you will have when you use it.

To help answer the question above, consider the following focus questions:

Was your moment the loss of a loved one? If so, you may be a Loss Overcomer.

Was your moment a betrayal by someone you trusted? If so, you may be a Betrayal Overcomer.

Was your moment a personal or business failure? If so, you may be a Failure Overcomer.

Was your moment a traumatic event? If so, you may be a Trauma Overcomer.

Was your moment a time when you felt rejected or not good enough? If so, you may be a Rejection Overcomer.

The Transformative Power of Thankfulness

Your transformation requires a before and after. Before a tree was a tree, it was a seed. Before a butterfly was a butterfly, it was a caterpillar. Transformation is only possible when a before becomes an after. Most people live in the "before" part of their transformation. Very few live in the "after." Purpose Factor people live in the after.

If you're going to experience transformation, you must reframe how you think about your Origin Story. Neuroscientist Kevin Ochsner at Columbia University says you can learn how to reframe the negative moments in your life. You can reframe a negative into a positive, or an emotional response into a logical one. See? Before and after.

If you believe that your childhood holds you back, it will. If you believe a divorce makes you unlovable, it will. But, if you reframe the way you look at your Origin Story, you can transform your negative thinking into a positive impact on others.

Once you know your Origin Story, you can choose to look at it one of two ways: with bitterness or gratefulness.

When you think about the moment that most shaped you, it may cause you to get upset. You may think about the person or people that hurt you. Your heart may race, your palms may sweat, and your jaw may clench tight. While no one would blame you for feeling that way, living that way forever does you no good—especially if you want to use your Purpose Factor. It's impossible to start helping others when you can't stop thinking about what others have done to you. The secret to overcoming your Origin Story is to transform your bitterness into gratefulness.

A good friend of ours is a successful young professional. To us, he always seemed content with his life and career.

That was until we helped him understand his Origin Story. When we asked him, "Early in life, which moment or series of moments most shaped the way you see the world?" his answer left us in tears.

This impressive man was raised in a good family, but his father struggled with anger. No matter what he did, he could never please his father. Sometimes, he said his father would get violent and throw him around. His father's actions often scared his mom and siblings. It became clear that our friend had never talked through his father's anger. After he told the story, Brian asked a question that would change everything. "Why are you thankful for what happened to you?"

You could have heard a pin drop. Thankful? He had been physically and emotionally abused by the one person who was supposed to protect him. Was he supposed to be glad that happened? Brian let the question hang in the air until he responded. Our friend finally said, "I'm grateful because that moment showed me the kind of man I don't want to be. It made me want to protect people, especially women."

What happened to you or because of you doesn't have to hold you back. You can use it to help others with whatever they're going through. Our friend was able to turn his trauma into a desire to help others. Like him, when you choose gratefulness over bitterness, your Origin Story will give you clarity as to who you are, who you want to become, and who you want to help.

Your Story Is Your Authority

In addition to perspective, your Origin Story gives you authority. When you've overcome something, you have the authority to help others overcome. Whether you've overcome obesity, sexual assault, divorce, rejection, or financial ruin, those moments gave you the power and the insight to help others.

Patrik Baboumian was born in Iran in 1979 when the country was in the middle of regime change. He was four years old when his father, mother, and baby sister were in a terrible car accident. Only he and his mother survived. Eventually, he and his mother left Iran and moved to Germany to escape the political upheaval. That is the first part of his Origin Story.

In Germany, their landlord raised bunnies for food. Patrik can still remember a single moment that shaped his view of the world: when he was still a kid, Patrik saw the same landlord throw a baby bunny against the wall and break its neck. Then the landlord threw the helpless creature away. Patrik's formative years made him want to defend the defenseless. He felt helpless to protect his family from the car crash and that bunny from being killed, but he didn't have to be helpless forever. At age fourteen, he became obsessed with getting strong. For years, Patrik perfected his skills in weight lifting and bodybuilding. He stopped eating meat and started advocating for animals. In 2011, he became the strongest man in Germany and has gone on to set world records as an all-vegan strongman.

Patrik's Natural Advantage as an Overseer showed him where to start, caring for people and animals. His top Acquired Skill as a Craftsman in bodybuilding and strength training defined his value in the marketplace. His Pull-Passion as an Injustice Equalizer gave him the motivation to become a vegan advocate. But more than anything, his Origin Story as a Loss Overcomer gave him both the perspective and the authority he needed to live out his Purpose Factor.

Once you discover your Origin Story, one of two things will happen. First, you'll want to drop everything and only help people with the same Origin Story. You will be deeply touched by what you have overcome and you will want to help others experience the kind of breakthrough you now have. While that sounds like the right thing to do, it may not be. This is not the part of the process where you quit your job and start a nonprofit. This is where you consider each element of your Purpose Factor in context of the others. Like Pull-Passion, following Origin Story alone will not bring fulfillment and meaning. Always consider your Origin Story with your Natural Advantage, Acquired Skills, and Pull-Passion.

Second, you might think that your Origin Story is too personal or obscure to help others. Your situation may be unique, but that moment gave you a platform and a perspective to help others overcome their specific challenges. Never doubt your authority or ability to help others experience breakthrough.

You've now discovered all four elements of your Purpose Factor. In the next section, you will discover how to combine them to help others and experience maximum personal fulfillment.

So what kind of Origin Story do you have? Are you a Loss Overcomer, Betrayal Overcomer, Failure Overcomer, Trauma Overcomer, or Rejection Overcomer?

My Origin Story is:

____.

My Natural Advantage:
I am a ______________________.

My Acquired Skill:
I am a ______________________.

My Pull-Passion:
I am a ______________________.

My Origin Story:
I am a ______________________
Overcomer.

Part Four

The Action: Steps to Living a Fulfilled Life

Introduction

When we started on our journey, we realized we would never be successful using our purpose without a system. If it took a system to find our purpose, it would take a system to use our purpose. We started studying the methods, systems, and strategies of great leaders, movements, and social trends. The more stories we read, the more patterns emerged.

It didn't matter who we were looking at; they all had three things in common:

1. They started with people.
2. They addressed a problem.
3. They created a solution.

As we dug deeper, we noticed that it wasn't just a system that made them successful. It was the sequence. It was the right elements in the right order for the right reason.

The secret is the sequence.

Follow the right sequence, and you will use your Purpose Factor to make an incredible impact. You will finally understand who you are, who you can help, and how you can help them with what you have.

There is a system for living out your Purpose Factor, and when followed, you unlock a powerful and fulfilling life. The sequence is simple: people, problem, solution. When followed intentionally, and in that order, your Purpose Factor is unlocked and ready to use.

Your Origin Story indicates the people you were made to help. Your Pull-Passion influences the kind of problem you can solve. Your Natural Advantage and Acquired Skills point to the solution that you are best equipped to deliver.

There is a problem with only discovering your purpose. Knowing does not equal doing. Without knowing how to use your Purpose Factor, you get stuck in a cycle where you're frustrated with your situation, clueless about what's next, and making decisions not knowing what's the right move.

A philanthropist friend of ours has a phrase for when this happens: "You're all dressed up with nowhere to go." It's a funny phrase with a hidden message. It means being ready for something to happen, but then nothing happens. The same is true with discovering purpose. You do the hard work of finding your purpose, but without doing anything with it, you're dressed up sitting on your living room couch.

People who lose weight but don't adopt a system to keep it off gain the weight back. People who get out of debt but don't save will find themselves in the same financial wreck again. To make something last, we must have a system. To make the system work, we need to follow a sequence.

This section is all about *who* you will help with your Purpose Factor—and how you will help them. No more wondering. No more waiting. Just an epiphany-like moment where everything starts to come together.

Your purpose is your permission.

15

The People You Were Made to Help

"You can get everything in life you want, if you will just help enough other people get what they want." —**Zig Ziglar**

The 1936 edition of *Popular Mechanics* introduced a bizarre new weapon of war. It was called the "Tumbleweed Tank." The inventor was a Texan by the name of A.J. Richardson, and he was determined to design a militarized vehicle that protected the soldiers inside.

In the magazine, there was an illustration of the Tumbleweed Tank. Readers could even see a cutaway view of the interior. The proposed death machine was a round metal orb. It was designed to cross terrain that other tanks couldn't. It came equipped with two machine guns, protection against poisonous gas, and an anti-aircraft gun. The tank seemed to address every vulnerability.

The only problem? There were no windows—no way to determine which direction to drive or shoot. Despite his effort to produce an unstoppable weapon of war, A.J. failed to consider something very important.

He failed to think about who would actually use the Tumbleweed Tank.

If you read the *Popular Mechanics* article, it becomes obvious that A.J. thought about the Tumbleweed's "why" and its "how," but not its "who." If he had started with who (the soldiers), he may have thought, "The soldiers would probably like to know which way they're driving and shooting." It's safe to say the Tumbleweed Tank never made it to the battlefield.

When we started on this journey together, we told you that discovering and living out your Purpose Factor is about answering this two-part question: Who am I, and who am I supposed to help? In the last section, by helping you discover the four elements of your Purpose Factor, we answered the first question, "Who am I?"

Now we'll answer the second question, "Who am I supposed to help?" Like A.J. and the Tumbleweed Tank, you can get the *what*, *why*, and *how* right. But if you get the *who* wrong, you'll lose. You'll end up driving all over the place and shooting in all the wrong directions.

In other words, it's not enough to know the problem you can solve and the solution you can craft. You must first know *who* has the problem before you can craft the right solution. When you start with who, everything falls into place.

Start with Who

When we got our start in business, we made the same mistake as A.J. We made business all about us and the question "What can we sell?" instead of "Who can we help?" Our priorities were backward and it cost us big. We wasted thousands of dollars and hundreds of hours creating products that no one wanted. Making a single sale was like getting a root canal without anesthetic. The harder we worked, the less money we made. We seemed to be going in the opposite direction of success.

That's because when you craft a solution to a problem without first getting to know who the solution is for, you make a big assumption. You assume that your solution is the one that people want. Though you could be right, you're more likely wrong. That's like a doctor prescribing medication to a patient without asking questions or doing an exam. How can you know what to prescribe without finding out who it's for?

When our bad sales numbers forced us back to the drawing board, we started asking the right question, "Who are we supposed to help?" As it turns out, we weren't the first to ask this question.

When you look closely, you realize that every problem is a people problem. Whether it's protecting the environment or repealing bad laws, every problem you encounter and every solution you develop impacts people. So why not start with the people you're meant to help? Why not start with "who"?

Nearly every religion teaches something similar. Jesus taught the most important commandments were to love God and love others. Buddhism teaches its followers to love all beings as a mother protecting an only child. The Torah tells you to love your neighbor as yourself.

Pop culture echoes these truths. We know it's better to give than receive, and as children, we're taught the Golden Rule. When it comes to living out these principles, however, we do the opposite. We live for ourselves. We fail to ask, "Who are we supposed to help?"

But when we ask, "Who?" first, we put a face to the problem we were made to solve.

Where to Start

Some folks already have extreme clarity as to who they want to help. You may want to help busy moms, children without access to quality education, or doctors experiencing burnout. Others need more help determining their *who*.

To know who you're supposed to help, it's best to start with your Origin Story. Your Origin Story is the moment that most shaped the way you see the world. That moment reveals the people who need your help overcoming what you have already overcome.

Your *who* can be the people you relate to most. You see your story in their story. Financial guru Suze Orman lost $52,000 of her friend's money on her first investment. She used her Failure Overcomer story to help women who are new to personal finance.

Your *who* can also be the people you're most drawn to help. Though their story is not your story, there's something about their life that reminds you of yours.

Dr. Martin Luther King, Jr.'s *who* were fellow African Americans being treated like second-class citizens. Viola Gregg Liuzzo shared Dr. King's *who*, but she looked nothing like him. Viola was a white housewife from Detroit. Her Origin Story was shaped when she saw racial inequality as a small child. Her family was extremely poor, living in a one-room shack with no running water. Despite their poverty, Viola noticed that her family was treated better than African Americans in the segregated South.

In March of 1965, Viola traveled from Detroit to Alabama to volunteer with Dr. King. On the evening of March 25, Viola was driving a young African American civil rights activist home when she was shot and killed by the Ku Klux Klan. The young man only survived by pretending to be dead. The thirty-nine-year-old mother of five was the only white female to have died during the civil rights movement.

Viola's life proves that you don't have to be like the people you serve, but you do need to like them. Your *who* are the people you serve, no matter where they come from or what they look like.

How to Discover Your Who

The moment you discover your *who* is the moment you discover how to experience fulfillment. Remember, if your Purpose Factor is what you have to help others, fulfillment is the result of helping others with what you have. Fulfillment requires you to grow and give. If you're living out your Purpose Factor, you'll automatically grow and give what you have to help others. Consider the following questions to discover *who* you're supposed to help:

QUESTION 1: IF YOU COULD ONLY HELP ONE TYPE OF PERSON, WHO WOULD YOU HELP?

In helping people discover their *who*, we hear some great answers to this question. But sometimes we get the response "I want to help everyone." We call this the "Miss America" answer. It sounds nice, but it's not specific enough to focus your action or create a helpful solution. Do you get just as much joy helping a friend move apartments as you do helping someone with their taxes? Do you enjoy helping a small business strategize about social media just as much as you enjoy helping discouraged parents relate to their teenagers? Of course you don't. Instead, it's best to consider your Origin Story and look for people who need to overcome what you already have.

QUESTION 2: WHAT ABOUT THAT PERSON'S LIFE MOST RESONATES WITH YOU?

One of the best ways to get clarity on your *who* is to determine why you're drawn to help them. If you can't relate to or see yourself in your *who*, you'll not only lack in motivation; you'll lack in empathy.

To help you see how your Origin Story reveals your *who*, we'll consider three different people. We'll use their Purpose Factor to identify who they're supposed to help.

Sara is a real estate agent in Newport Beach, California, whose Natural Advantage is a Recruiter. She loves sharing her favorite brands, experiences, and beliefs with others. Her top Acquired Skills are in selling luxury houses and online marketing—specifically, Facebook marketing. That makes her a Messenger. Her Pull-Passion is a Need Satisfier, which is evident when she helps new families settle in the area. Sara hates to see families have bad experiences with real estate agents. As for her Origin Story, Sara is a Rejection Overcomer. She experienced the hurt of her dad walking out, leaving Sara and her mom to fend for themselves.

As a Rejection Overcomer, Sara looks for opportunities to make people feel included. As a real estate agent, this inspires her to find homes for families new to Newport Beach.

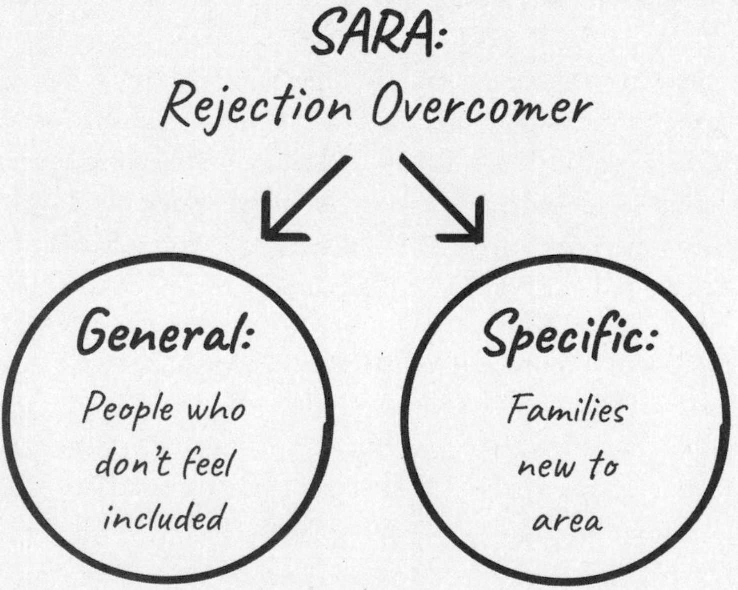

John is an accountant in Pittsburgh, Pennsylvania. John's Natural Advantage is a Teacher. He is always sharing what he's learned or how he does things. His Acquired Skills in risk analysis and accounting make him a Protector, and his Pull-Passion is a Problem Solver. He's always looking for problems to solve around the house, in his community, or at the company. It bothers him when others don't address issues that should be obvious. John's Origin Story is a Betrayal Overcomer. His wife left him a year into their marriage for his high school best friend.

As a Betrayal Overcomer, John is the stable, reliable person at home and on the job. His ex-wife's betrayal shifted his perspective by giving him the ability to help others overcome instability. This influences who John mentors, who are usually employees who have lost faith in their company.

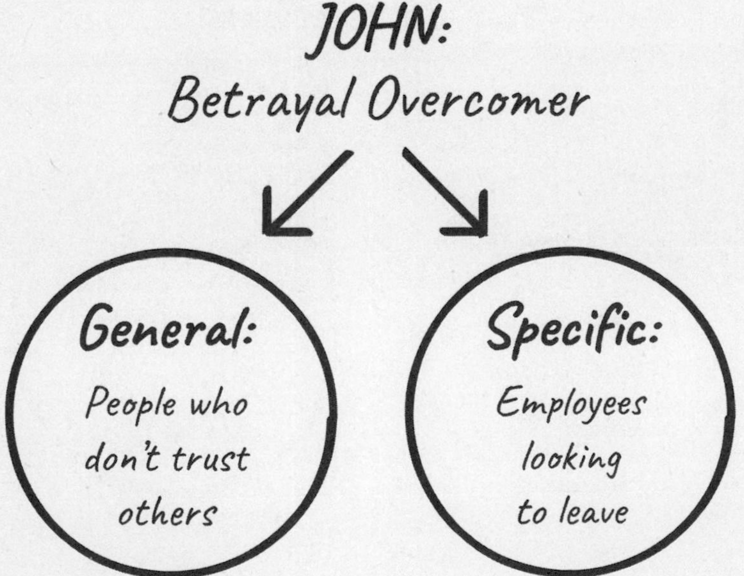

Carlos is a college student studying to be a graphic designer in Boise, Idaho. Carlos's Natural Advantage is an Overseer. He's always making sure that others are included in group projects. Carlos's Acquired Skills are still being formed, but as a future graphic designer, he is developing skills as a Messenger. Carlos's Pull-Passion is Hurt Healer, which came from his Origin Story as a Trauma Overcomer. When he was a kid, Carlos was in a bad car accident and lost mobility in one of his arms. He knows how hard it is to overcome physical limitations to reach goals.

Carlos's Trauma Overcomer story gets him excited about helping others overcome adversity. He is most drawn to helping those with physical challenges see their disabilities as opportunities.

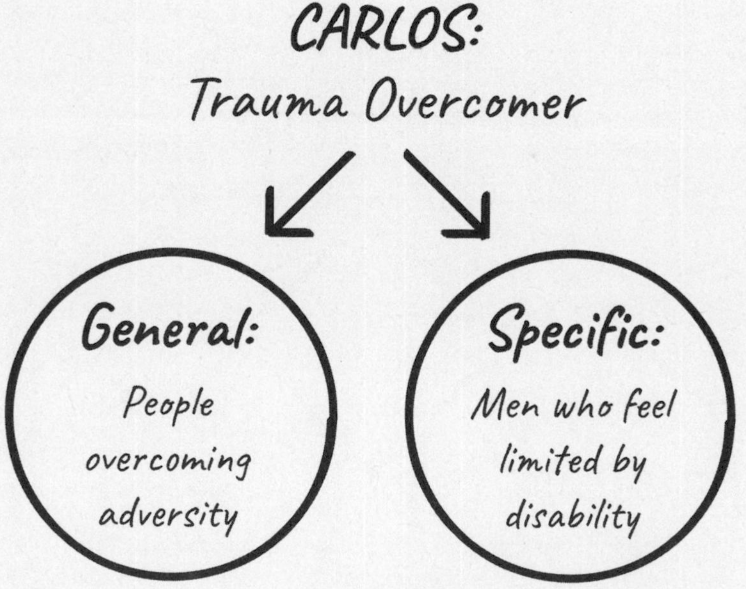

Generally, It's Specific

When Carlos graduates college, he may discover that his *who* is too specific. He may struggle to find a company with a role that serves men who feel limited by disability. But by making his *who* more general, he could find a role helping more people overcome adversity. Perhaps on the side, he could start an online community for young men with disabilities.

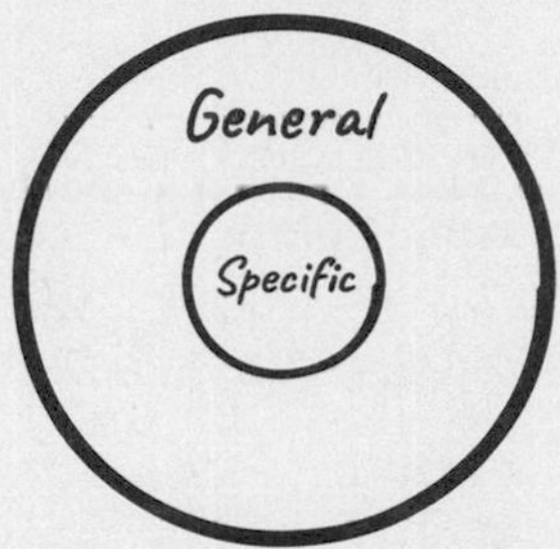

Your Origin Story will help you correctly identify who you're supposed to help. You can broaden or narrow your audience definition depending on your goals or job description. For example, Brian's Origin Story as a Trauma Overcomer makes him empathetic towards victims of sexual abuse. But he has defined his *who* more broadly. His *who* are people who don't know their Purpose Factor. By helping a broad group of people discover their Purpose Factor, he can also help victims of sexual abuse overcome their pasts.

To decide whether your *who* should be general or specific, ask yourself the following questions:

1. Are there enough people in my *who* that I can help? If you're too specific, there may not be enough people to benefit from your solution. If your *who* is too general, people may feel your solution doesn't apply to them.

2. How many people do I want to impact with my Purpose Factor? The more people you want to impact, the more general you'll need to be.

Your Success Starts with Who

The most successful among us ask, "Who am I supposed to help?" Sam Walton, the founder of Walmart, started with *who*: his customers. Sam exclaimed, "There is only one boss: the customer. And he can fire everybody in the company from the chairman on down, simply by spending his money somewhere else."

Thomas Edison started with *who*: the people of modern society. Thomas said, "I find out what the world needs. Then I go ahead and try to invent it." Henry Ford started with a *who* he could relate to: working-class families who couldn't afford expensive automobiles. Whether it's cheaper dish soap or electricity, all great inventions, movements, and services start with *who*.

Using your Purpose Factor to help people by solving problems, satisfying needs, healing hurts, fulfilling desires, and equalizing injustices begins and ends with *who*. Where there are people to help, there are problems to solve.

The People I Was Made to Help:

____.

16

The Problem You Were Designed to Solve

"All life is problem solving." —***Karl Popper***

Everything in life comes down to solving problems. The economy is about solving problems. Every business, invention, and movement got its start by solving a problem. Helping others is about solving problems. When your Purpose Factor is what you have to help others, then living it out is about helping others by solving problems.

We spent the last chapter answering the question "Who am I supposed to help?" for a simple reason. Picking the problem in the world you were made to solve is overwhelming when you don't know your "who." You wonder, "Which problem? Where do I start? How much of the problem can I solve right now?"

For most, it's better to pick the people before picking the problem. By first asking, "Who?" and then asking, "What?" it's easier to determine the problem you were made to solve. Now that you know your "who," you must identify your "what," which is the problem your Purpose Factor best equips you to solve. To do that, we must return to your Pull-Passion.

Start with Your Pull-Passion

Your Pull-Passion is the problem in the world that you're made to solve. The word problem can also mean need, hurt, desire, or injustice. For example, if your Pull-Passion is Hurt Healer, then your problem is the hurt in the world that you're made to heal.

Or, if it's Need Satisfier, then your problem is the need in the world that you're made to satisfy.

You may also remember that your Pull-Passion is your motivation. It pulls you out of bed and drives you to help people with what you have. When you know your Pull-Passion, you know how to pick the problem that you're made to solve. You know how to choose your "what."

Need Satisfiers solve problems by helping people meet their needs. This could include assisting others to find jobs, get healthy food, or gain access to healthcare. Need Satisfiers are passionate about helping their "who" get what they need to live and thrive.

Hurt Healers solve problems by helping people heal from emotional and physical pain. This could include counseling someone through an addiction, coaching someone overcoming an eating disorder, or helping someone feel more confident after a mastectomy. Hurt Healers are passionate about helping their "who" become whole again.

Desire Fulfillers solve problems by helping people experience joy. This could include creating world-class entertainment, improving product design, or designing sustainable clothing. Desire Fulfillers are passionate about giving their "who" an excellent experience.

Injustice Equalizers solve problems by helping people get justice. They are passionate about righting wrongs. This could include cleaning up the environment or advocating for disenfranchised people groups.

Problem Solvers solve problems by helping people do things bigger, faster, or more efficiently. They're passionate about asking big-picture questions and helping people eliminate the obstacles to getting things done. This could be teaching an online entrepreneurship course or creating sterile surgery pods that can be used in third-world conditions.

Questions for Discovering the Problem You're Made to Solve

The more you understand your "what," the more you'll be able to create the solution. There are two questions for discovering the problem that your Purpose Factor has built you to solve.

Consider the following:

1. WHAT PROBLEM HAVE YOU SOLVED FOR YOURSELF THAT YOU WOULD LOVE TO SOLVE FOR OTHERS?

Some of the world's greatest problem solvers started out by solving a problem for themselves. Remember that Sara Blakely invented Spanx after creating the first pair for herself when she couldn't find shapewear that she liked. What problem have you solved for yourself? Maybe you beat cancer, sold your last company for $50 million, or found the best places to buy organic baby food. If you've done these things for yourself, there's a good chance you can do them for others.

When you solve a problem for yourself, you gain experience and develop expertise. In other words, your experience in solving the problem for yourself gives you the authority to solve it for others.

2. WHAT PROBLEM ARE YOU MOST PASSIONATE ABOUT SOLVING?

Your Pull-Passion is the problem in the world that you were made to solve. Of the issues in the world that you could address, which one bothers you the most? Which one makes you think, "If I could just fix this one problem, I would know my life mattered?"

There are only two types of problems in the world: current problems that need to be solved and future problems that need to be prevented. Problems that need to be prevented include helping people avoid pain, whereas problems that need a solution now help people alleviate pain. For example, your Pull-Passion may show that you want to help end human trafficking. If you like preventing problems before they start, you could create campaigns that raise awareness and pass laws to stop trafficking at the source. If you like solving problems that already exist, you could help by prosecuting traffickers or building safe houses for victims. Get specific about the types of problems you are best equipped to solve and nothing will hold you back.

Rules for Picking Your Problem

1. Get Specific

Albert Einstein is quoted as saying, "If I were given one hour to save the planet, I would spend fifty-nine minutes defining the problem and one minute resolving it." Getting specific worked for him, and it will work for you, too.

The more clarity you have about the problem you were made to solve for your "who," the more you'll be able to help them. Mediocre focus leads to mediocre results. Extraordinary focus leads to extraordinary results.

There is a well-known phrase in internet marketing that says, "The riches are in the niches." The most successful companies and people start with a well-defined niche, or "who," and a well-defined problem. Amazon helped people buy and sell books before expanding into an internet shopping superpower.

Comedian Kevin Hart started his career doing stand-up comedy about his experience as a black man in America before starring in box-office hits. Mary Kay Ash built her makeup empire by helping local women succeed in business.

As you close in on the problem you were made to solve, you'll see how knowing your "who" helps you get more specific. And by defining your problem specifically, you'll be able to craft your solution easily.

2. Ask Questions

According to Richard Branson, "Solving problems means listening." If you don't know the problem your Purpose Factor equipped you to solve, start by asking questions. By asking your "who" questions and listening to their answers, you'll get to know how you can help them better.

In our own lives, we ask two questions when we're thinking about solving a problem for *our* "who," people who don't know their purpose. These questions will work for you, too. The first question is "What's the biggest challenge you are facing right now?" and the second question is "What do you believe is holding you back the most right now?"

The words "biggest" and "right now" in these questions help us determine how we can help our "who" the most, by solving what they care about. The words also help us decide how we can help our "who" the soonest, by solving their most pressing problem. It also helps us determine if we need more information or more skills to best serve them.

When William Wilberforce wanted to abolish slavery in England, he began by listening. His Pull-Passion was Problem Solver; he was drawn to solving a big societal issue. But to know how he could help the most, he had to educate himself. To do that,

William sought out the guidance of John Newton, a former slave ship captain turned clergyman who wrote the hymn "Amazing Grace." William asked John questions, and John answered them. This helped William specifically define the problem so he could specifically design his solution.

No matter the type of problem you want to solve, your journey to use your Purpose Factor always starts by asking questions.

3. Make It Personal

The key to passionate work is solving a problem you've personally experienced—or at least one you can relate to. When Chuck Templeton couldn't get a restaurant reservation, it caused him to start OpenTable, the restaurant reservation app.

Reflecting on how the company got started, Chuck explained:

> *One weekend my in-laws were visiting, and my wife wanted to make restaurant reservations. She ended up spending three and a half hours calling restaurant after restaurant. I thought it would be great to build a website that could hook up to back-end restaurant reservation terminals.*

If that weekend nightmare had never happened, he would have never created the app. If that app wasn't created, many of us would still be spending hours on the phone trying to get reservations.

Chuck picked a problem he personally experienced and has helped thousands of people have better dining experiences. If you don't pick a problem you can at least relate to, you won't care about the problem, much less work hard enough to make the solution. Consider what you talk most about with friends and family. Is there something that you consistently bring up that bothers you or an opportunity that excites you? Or is the problem one you have to force yourself to get excited about? Do you see yourself in the people who have this problem, or do you find it hard to relate to them? The more personal the problem is for you, the more pulled you will be to solve it.

4. Take It One Problem at a Time

If we have one point of caution, it's this: some people fail by trying to solve too many problems all at once. Though well-intentioned, it's not effective and leads to frustration. Successful people know the secret to having a big impact is starting small. Professional jugglers, project managers, and parents will tell you it's hard to focus on more than one big problem at a time. Pick the one problem you have the resources and relationships to begin solving now. Then, as your impact grows, go bigger.

The video games we played as kids were designed in levels. At the end of each level was a boss that you had to defeat. Fail, and you had to start over. Win, and you got to continue. You couldn't beat the entire game on the first level. The same is true with picking the problem you were made to solve. Take it one level at a time.

Putting It to Work

Let's bring back our friends, Sara, John, and Carlos, to help them get clarity on the problems they were made to solve.

Sara's Pull-Passion is Need Satisfier, which means she wants everyone she meets to have an incredible experience. Her Pull-Passion highlights the problem she is made to solve: helping her clients enjoy the home-buying process from beginning to end.

SARA:
Need Satisfier
↓
Real Estate Agent
↓
Helping families find
the perfect luxury home

John's Pull-Passion is Problem Solver, which means he is passionate about finding new and better ways to solve big problems. The problems that John solves are often tied to his job, but you can see his problem-solving mind at home too. He uses his Pull-Passion to research issues, consider new solutions, and challenge the outdated ways of getting things done.

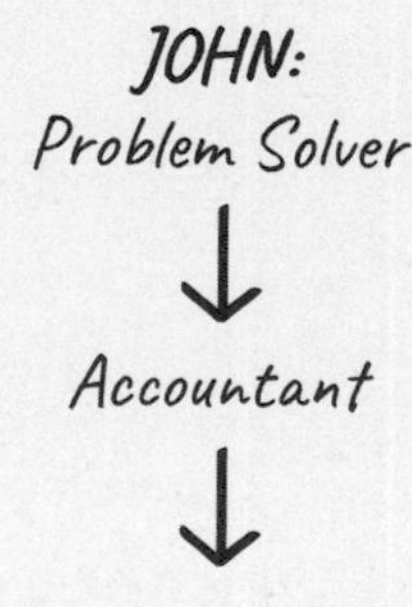

Reducing waste and increasing
efficiency for growing companies

Carlos's Pull-Passion is Hurt Healer. When he sees people that don't feel included, either because of a disability or because they're different, it bothers him. His Pull-Passion makes him passionate about helping people that feel rejected because they aren't like everyone else.

CARLOS:
Hurt Healer
↓
Graphic Design Student
↓
Creating diverse, inclusive project teams within design companies

The discovery and application of purpose have never been so easy or so linear. We've made the path to discovering and living out your Purpose Factor simple and straightforward. Your first step was to discover your "who" by looking for the people you were made to help. We just finished the second step, discovering your "what," defining the problem your Purpose Factor best equipped you to solve. Next, you'll discover your "how," the solution you were made to create.

The Problem I Was Designed to Solve:

____.

17

The Solution You Are Prepared to Deliver

"You're either part of the solution or you're part of the problem."
—Eldridge Cleaver

Admit it. You've been sucked in by one of those infomercials for workout equipment. So have we. A celebrity trainer takes over your television and says, "Have you ever wanted abs like these? Now you can have abs like these in less than fifteen minutes a day!" Additionally, they promise, "It's not only easy to use. It also fits under your bed!" Of course, it comes with a free cookbook.

Aside from the outlandish promises and actors using the product without sweating, what do all these infomercials have in common?

They are all stories of transformation.

Before and after pictures and testimonials splash across the screen. One happy customer, with both legs inside one pant leg of an old pair of pants says, "I used to look like this and now I look like this!" Another customer, a guy in his mid-fifties, is on vacation with his wife rocking the abs of a twenty-five-year-old.

Hidden in the script of these cheesy marketing masterpieces is an important truth: **great solutions must transform lives**.

Chapter after chapter, paragraph after paragraph, we have said that your Purpose Factor is what you have to *help others*. But what do we mean by "help others"?

Using your Purpose Factor to help others is about giving the people you were made to help a *transformation*. Just like the testimonials in the infomercials, you must give your "who" a "before and after" experience.

They once bought terrible food for their kids, but after reading your blog, now they know how to feed their kids right on a budget. They were in the depths of depression, but after working with you, now they view setbacks as opportunities. Their production lines were slow because of bad equipment, but after buying new technology from you, their profit is up and costs are down.

Now that you know the people you were made to help and the problem you were made to solve, you must design the solution you were made to create.

When designing your solution, you must first ask, "What do I have to help solve the problem?" The answer is found in your Natural Advantage and Acquired Skills. Your Natural Advantage is the role you tend to play in life and work. It's also your head start in a world full of competing solutions.

Your Acquired Skills are abilities you attained through school, training, and experience. They are the tools and tricks you've developed over your life. The solution you create to help your "who" will represent a combination of your Natural Advantage and Acquired Skills.

To begin thinking about your solution, consider the following:

1. How has your Natural Advantage gifted you to solve the problem?
2. How have your Acquired Skills equipped you to solve the problem?

Helping by Focusing

Eric Sevareid, the late CBS news reporter, pointed out that "the chief cause of problems is solutions." We would add, "A problem with too many solutions becomes a bigger problem."

When using your Purpose Factor to help your "who," your solution must represent the simplest, shortest path to transformation. Many people go too big too fast in the excitement of discovering their Purpose Factor, the people they were made to help, and the problem they were made to solve. They attempt to solve the problem with twenty different solutions instead of creating the one solution that makes the most difference.

The biggest brands in the world started with one solution to one problem or one satisfaction to one desire. McDonald's started with hamburgers. Domino's started with pizza. Even The Cheesecake Factory, known for its massive menu, had humble beginnings with only cheesecakes—sold from Evelyn Overton's basement in Detroit, Michigan. It was only after her success in one thing that they created many things.

The more specific and singular the solution, the bigger the transformation.

As an example, let's say the problem you want to solve is bad customer service at hotels. As for your Natural Advantage, you're the Builder. You love to design and launch things. You have Acquired Skills in hospitality, specifically as a Messenger training hotel staff on providing a consistent customer experience.

While it's tempting to create an app for customers and managers to rate hotel staff, that would be too much too soon—costing too much money and development time. Given your Origin Story of overcoming a major early-career failure, you know your "who." It's hotel employees. After listening to your "who," you combine your Natural Advantage and Acquired Skills to create a dynamic, customer-experience training program. As a result of your program, your clients' online reviews are through the roof. On the back of the program's success, you then build the app, which will allow you to grow your impact.

You see? It's like washing your hair. Lather, rinse, and repeat. But in this case, it's people, problem, solution. Then repeat.

Does Your Solution Fit?

We all know what it's like to try on clothes. If a shirt is too big or small, we won't buy it. The same is true when creating a solution to the problem you were made to solve for the people you were made to help. If it doesn't fit, they won't buy it.

One of our friends is a tech titan and angel investor. While most entrepreneurs can only hope to sell one company in their lifetime, he has sold two. Through his experience, he has sharpened his ability to identify successful solutions. In all of our interactions, we can't remember a conversation in which he didn't talk about "product-market fit."

Yes, it's one of those semi-scientific-sounding terms well above our reading level. So for our sake and yours, we'll keep it simple. Product-market fit is about creating a solution that meets the actual needs of your "who," and doing it better than the competition. In other words, do you have a solution that helps people better than anything else? And does that solution help them how they want to be helped?

Below are some product-market-fit questions that we've borrowed from the business world to help you get extreme clarity on the solution you were made to create.

1. Who else is solving the problem? Never assume that you have the only solution. If the problem is as real as you believe it to be, there's likely someone else trying to solve it.

2. How are the other solutions failing to serve people? Perhaps the other solutions are too expensive, too complicated, or not customized to their needs.
3. How can you offer a better solution? What will make your solution stand out in its ability to transform people?

In the classic business book *Blue Ocean Strategy*, business gurus W. Chan Kim and Renée Mauborgne relay that if you want to create a successful solution, you must set yourself apart. As an example, maybe you want to offer childcare in your neighborhood. How will you be better than the preschool down the street? Is there something you can do that the preschool can't? Maybe you want to eliminate duplicative systems in your company. How will your solution be better than the current system? What challenges will you have to overcome to get others to adopt the new approach?

To show you exactly how to do this, let's bring back Sara, John, and Carlos to help them discover their solution.

Sara's Natural Advantage as a Recruiter makes her the perfect real estate agent. Beyond the sale, she shares decorating tips, great places to eat, and is a networking queen. Her Acquired Skills as a Messenger help her communicate in person and online.

After discovering her Purpose Factor, Sara creates an online guide and video channel for families interested in moving to Southern California. When you combine Sara's people, problem, and solution with her Purpose Factor, it looks like this:

I help families new to Southern California (people) with finding a new home (problem) by creating interesting, useful content that enables them to make the right decision (solution).

John's Natural Advantage as a Teacher means he is always helping people better understand their financial goals. His

Acquired Skills as an accountant make him the Protector, which is someone who takes care of the details and reduces risk. Specifically, because John has expertise in simultaneously analyzing risk for multiple clients, he helps his colleagues do the same. After finding his Purpose Factor, John creates a program to teach his system for analyzing risk to new and at-risk employees. When you combine John's people, problem, and solution with his Purpose Factor, it looks like this:

I help new and frustrated employees (people) with finding more efficient ways to serve their clients (problem) by teaching them the best system to help clients and add value to the company (solution).

Carlos's Natural Advantage as an Overseer means that he wants to be sure others are taken care of. His Acquired Skills in graphic design make him a Messenger. When you combine Carlos's people, problem, and solution with his Purpose Factor, it looks like this:

I help young men who feel defined by their setbacks (people) with feeling included and valued (problem) by designing motivational materials that help them overcome their setbacks (solution).

Sara, John, and Carlos were able to use the elements of their Purpose Factor to discover who they are, who they can help, and how to experience maximum fulfillment. The process is clear and the steps are simple. It's up to you to take the action to turn your Purpose Factor into impact.

The solution you were made to deliver is unique to you. It is the perfect combination of who you are, what you've overcome, and what you can provide. We're not going for mediocre solutions. You were designed to create extraordinary solutions that lead to extraordinary results. When you take the time to dig into your Acquired Skills and your Natural Advantage to create a solution, you will live out what many only dream of achieving. You will be using your Purpose Factor to make a living and make a difference.

The Solution I Am Prepared to Deliver:

____.

I help _____________________________
(People) with

____

(Problem) by

____

(Solution) because
I am a _____________________________
Overcomer
(Origin Story).

18

The Life You Were Meant to Live

Is it possible to know your Purpose Factor and not use it? Of course. Knowing does not equal doing. We know an apple is better than cake, but we still ask for the dessert menu. We know saving is better than spending, but we still open up another credit card. What we know does not translate into action until we adjust our mindset. To use our Purpose Factor to help others, we must address our mindsets, update our habits, and reset our expectations.

On our journey together, you first discovered your Purpose Factor. You got extreme clarity about who you are and how you can help people. Then you put your Purpose Factor to work by identifying the people you will help, the problem you will solve, and the solution you will provide. Now, you must design your life to support your Purpose Factor.

Winning the Battle in Your Brain

George Bernard Shaw wrote, "Progress is impossible without change, and those who cannot change their minds cannot change anything." In other words, change your mind, change your life. The only way to change your mind is by taking ownership of what's in your mind—your beliefs.

Everything we do in our lives comes down to beliefs. When we discovered this simple truth, we had instant clarity on why we hadn't seen results. It wasn't our goals that were bad. It was what we believed about our goals that held us back. We saw how our beliefs influenced everything—from not putting away the laundry to spending too much at dinner and how we reacted to family drama. No matter how hard we tried, no matter how much we wanted to improve, nothing changed until our beliefs changed.

No one is immune to the power of their beliefs. No one. Those beliefs, whether we chose them consciously or adopted them unconsciously, have defined how we see ourselves and how we use our Purpose Factor. There is a two-part truth that, when understood, will unlock how you use your Purpose Factor. **First, what we believe is what we act on. Second, we never act against our beliefs.**

Changing your actions starts with changing your beliefs. In order to turn your Purpose Factor into action, you must take ownership of what you believe.

Discovering your Purpose Factor is a process. Defining who you can help and how you can help them is a process. Identifying and replacing bad beliefs is a process as well.

Step One: Identify Your Beliefs

What you believe about something will determine how you act. What you believe about food will influence your diet. What you believe about love will influence your relationships. What you believe about forgiveness will influence how you treat others.

There are three categories of beliefs: 1) beliefs about yourself, 2) beliefs about others, and 3) beliefs about how the world works. Beliefs about yourself include your self-esteem, your perceived abilities, and your purpose. Beliefs about others include your expectations for them (more on expectations later) and what they do for you. Beliefs about the world include how you see the universe helping or hurting you.

Here are some example beliefs, both good and bad:

I believe that I have everything I need to be successful.
I believe that I am unlucky.
I believe that other people will betray me if given the chance.
I believe that people are mostly good.
I believe that you have to fight to get ahead.
I believe that opportunity is everywhere.

It's one thing to talk about what others believe. It's another to talk about what *we* believe.

Do this for us. Take out a piece of paper, a notebook, or wherever you keep things written down. Write out three to five beliefs under each category: 1) beliefs about yourself, 2) beliefs about others, and 3) beliefs about how the world works.

Consider each category one at a time and fill in your specific beliefs.

Beliefs about Yourself
How I handle my spiritual health...
How I approach my nutrition...
How I overcome rejection...
How I manage my time...

Beliefs about Others
How I handle my relationships...
How I let others influence me...
How I help others...
How I communicate with others...

Beliefs about the World
How I see opportunity...
How I view success...

How I view luck...

How I view failure...

Now consider the last twelve months. What beliefs helped you the most? What beliefs held you back? Now, go one step further, and look back at the last decade. What beliefs about yourself, others, and the world most influenced the way you lived and worked? If you do this right, this exercise should take ten to fifteen minutes to complete.

After identifying each belief, we move on to step two. This is where you will dismantle the belief by zeroing in on its impact in your life.

Step Two: Identify Their Impact

Once you have identified what you believe about yourself, what you believe about others, and what you believe about the world, you must identify the impact of those beliefs on your life. Are those beliefs helping you or hurting you?

One simple question, when answered, helps you decide if a belief is good or bad. It is the clarifying question that must guide every decision, every relationship, every job, and every opportunity.

The question goes like this: *Is this getting me closer to or further away from using my Purpose Factor?*

Print off this question and put it above your desk. Write it on a sticky note and place it in your notebook. Make it the background of your phone or desktop. Do whatever you need to do to remind yourself to only focus on what brings you closer to your purpose. Everything that falls outside of your Purpose Factor is a distraction. Everything that helps your Purpose Factor is your friend.

For example, we used to watch a lot of television. We identified what we believed about television. We believed we deserved to relax. That influenced what we thought about our time: we have time to watch television. That influenced our action: we watched lots of television.

By asking the question "Is this belief getting me closer to or further away from using my Purpose Factor?" we were able to adjust our actions. Our belief was good; we did need to relax. But we didn't ask ourselves if sitting on a couch and staring at a screen was the best way to relax. When we finished a movie, we didn't have more energy. We had less. So we adjusted our actions to find a more positive way to relax, like reading a book or going to the gym. Do we still watch television? Of course—we're normal people! But now it is less often and more focused. When you realize that every moment is getting you closer or further away from purpose, you even think about entertainment differently.

Go back to where you wrote down each of your beliefs. Take each category, one at a time, and where you wrote down your specific belief, ask the clarifying question. For example: "Does how I take care of my body get me closer to or further away from using my Purpose Factor?" Then, put a circle by the beliefs that are helping you use your Purpose Factor or an "X" by the beliefs that are not helping you use your Purpose Factor. After each belief, write down the impact (positive or negative) that belief has had on your life.

For example, "I believe that I have everything I need to be successful" is a good belief. Put a circle next to it. Then next to that belief, write down why it is good, such as "I feel confident about my future."

O *I believe that I have everything I need to be successful—I feel confident about my ability to solve problems.*

X *I believe that I am unlucky—I think good things can't happen to me.*

X *I believe that I can start a diet program whenever I want—I procrastinate on adopting healthy habits now.*

When you take the time to identify your bad beliefs and their negative effects, something powerful happens. The bad beliefs lose their grip on your mind. They are no longer subconscious thoughts. Now they are conscious thoughts that you can change from bad to good.

Step Three: Replace Bad Beliefs with Good Beliefs

Once you identify the bad beliefs keeping you from your Purpose Factor, you must replace them with good beliefs that power your Purpose Factor.

Go back to your list of beliefs. Create a new list of "good beliefs." On this list, write down all of the good beliefs from your past, as well as the good beliefs that are replacing your bad beliefs. Then, next to each good belief, explain how that good belief will help you.

O *I believe that I can make healthy decisions every day—I feel energized and am proud of the choices I make.*

O *I believe that I have everything I need to be successful—I feel confident about my ability to solve problems.*

O *I believe that I am in complete control of my future—I feel empowered to design the life I want.*

For example, you may incorrectly believe, "Nothing I do will be successful." Identify how that belief has hurt you: it has caused you to give up too early, doubt your ability, and fear risk. Next, you identify what helpful belief you must adopt to replace that bad belief. It could be, "Good things happen when I work hard" or "I have everything I need to be successful." With that new belief identified, you can then identify with an "I am" or "I feel" statement about how adopting that new belief will help you: "I am more confident; I will take more risks; I am committed to finishing projects."

One of the best ways to replace bad beliefs with good beliefs is with journaling. Why? Research shows that we can move things from our subconscious to our conscious mind by writing things down. At the beginning of this exercise, we encouraged you to write down your beliefs. We prefer journals because writing out our beliefs feels more reflective. Some prefer to use other forms of journaling, like an app on their phone. The key is to find a method that you like and will use daily.

Habit Overhaul

Most people think they need to change their habits to change their beliefs. They say, "If I go on a diet, then I won't think about food so much," or "If I worked out more, I would feel better about myself." So they keep trying to put new habits into old beliefs—like a round peg getting shoved into a square hole. It doesn't work. The most food-obsessed people we know are constantly dieting, and the most self-conscious people can work out five times a week. **It is not the action that determines your belief, it is the belief that determines your action.**

Your beliefs determine your habits. If you look at the habits of the successful, their beliefs are obvious. The same is true of those who do not live lives of impact. Habits are evidence of your beliefs. Once you have changed your beliefs from harmful to helpful, you can then change your habits.

A habit is a tendency to do something. By definition, habits are formed, which means they can be reformed if they don't serve your Purpose Factor. Not only do you have the ability to change your bad habits, you have the duty to change them.

There are five habit areas:

1. Faith. This includes religion, spirituality, and mindfulness.
2. Family. This includes friends, partners, and kids.
3. Finance. This includes saving, spending, and giving.
4. Health. This includes exercise, nutrition, and rest.
5. Work. This includes development, mastery, and fulfillment.

Within each of these five areas are three types of habits: 1) maintenance habits, 2) growth habits, and 3) destructive habits. Maintenance habits keep your life running, like paying your bills or getting your work done on time. Growth habits improve your life. These include taking your vitamins or going for a walk every morning. But destructive habits are those that distract you from your purpose. They include spending more money than you make or not getting good sleep.

Like beliefs, good habits are formed when bad habits are replaced. Bad habits are identified by asking the same clarifying question: *Is this getting me closer to or further away from using my Purpose Factor?*

Everyone has daily routines and weekly routines. Consider your routine and ask, "Does what I do in a typical day keep me from using my Purpose Factor?" Then consider, "Does what I do in a typical week keep me from using my Purpose Factor?" If you don't know off the top of your head, start by journaling a single day down to the fifteen minutes. Don't believe us? Do it tomorrow and see what your habits say about your priorities.

If your habits support using your Purpose Factor, keep them. If not, replace them. Like we did earlier in the chapter, we are now going to identify your helpful and harmful habits. Helpful habits fuel your purpose. Harmful habits distract you from your purpose.

In each of the five habit areas, write down your helpful habits and your harmful habits.

In my spiritual life, my helpful habits are...
My hurtful habits are...
In my family, my helpful habits are...
My hurtful habits are...
In how I handle my finances, my helpful habits are...
My hurtful habits are...
In my health routine, my helpful habits are...
My hurtful habits are...
In the work I do, my helpful habits are...
My hurtful habits are...

Next, you will identify good habits that will replace the bad habits. Like changing your beliefs, you do not delete a habit. You replace a habit.

For example, the habit you want to change is sleeping in past your alarm. Instead of simply setting the alarm one hour earlier to prevent the snooze (6:00 a.m. versus 7:00 a.m.), sign up for a cycling class at 6:30 a.m. Now you have a point of accountability and a new habit—the class. Maybe you have a bad habit of criticizing people. Instead of telling yourself to stop being critical, tell yourself one good thing you like about the other person. See? Bad habit replaced by good habit.

Here's the truth. You will never get rid of a bad habit without first replacing it with a good habit. No matter how hard you try or how positive you are, your mind will not delete, it can only replace. In your journal, take each category and write down the bad habit and the good habit that you are replacing it with.

My bad habit is ____.

The good habit I am replacing it with is

____.

The Secret Weapon of the Successful

You've identified your bad beliefs and bad habits and replaced them with good ones. Now you must have a system to keep yourself and your purpose on track. That system is daily confirmations.

Daily confirmations are how you align what you believe, how you feel, and what you do. The only way you will replace bad beliefs, harmful habits, and toxic threats is with daily confirmations.

We were skeptical at first. How could speaking the same thing every day make a difference in our life or our business? It sounded strange and it felt awkward, but we did it anyway. When we started using confirmations, everything changed. We were no longer reacting to life. Life was reacting to us. We were no longer disappointed in others or ourselves. We saw who we are and who we are here to help. In other words, we were finally in control of our lives.

In her confirmations, Gabrielle wrote down "getting a free trip to Hawaii." It happened three months later. She focused on getting a TEDx Talk and she received a phone call to do one a few months after that. Confirmations are proven to work. More than that, they are linked to lower stress, higher performance, and increases in physical activity.

Daily confirmations are simple statements that, when repeated, change how your brain processes information. Confirmations use "I have" and "I am" statements to rewire your brain. Daily confirmations have two parts: a belief statement and a statement about how that belief will make you feel. In other words, "I believe this, therefore I feel this."

The key to creating great confirmations is to choose statements that reflect your Purpose Factor. There is no point in repeating back a statement that is not aligned with who you are and who you can help. We didn't know this at first. When we initially practiced daily confirmations, we looked at what other people were doing. Their confirmations about fame and fortune became our confirmations. But their priorities weren't our priorities, so the confirmations didn't work. They made us feel worse about ourselves and frustrated with our purpose. Choose confirmations that represent the helpful beliefs and the helpful habits you are adopting.

Below are some of our daily confirmations:

I have the capacity to learn new skills, and I feel proud of my progress.

I love exercising, and I feel healthy and energized.

I am a quick learner, and I feel excited about the opportunity to improve myself.
I have enough time in the day to accomplish my goals, and I feel proud of my work at the end of every day.

We touch our confirmations every day. That could be writing them down in the morning, reviewing them at night, or listening to a recording of them while traveling. Daily confirmations work when done intentionally and consistently.

The most successful people in the world use daily confirmations to rewire their brains. They focus on their beliefs first and habits second. They don't spend all of their time fixing what's on the outside. They focus on the inside. They know what you now know: **your beliefs will determine if things happen to you or because of you.**

Turning your Purpose Factor into a lifestyle requires a system. That system starts with a belief reset and ends with supporting positive beliefs and habits through daily confirmations.

19

Setting Your Purpose Factor Goals

Finding your Purpose Factor started with asking "who." Using your Purpose Factor starts with asking "what." When it comes to using what you have to help others, your power comes from asking the right questions.

Most people never use their purpose because they never ask themselves, "What can I do to use my Purpose Factor?" In this book, you have discovered what your Purpose Factor is, who you are made to help, and how you can help them. Now, it's time to connect these steps to experience what less than 1 percent of the world experiences: maximum fulfillment and extreme clarity.

What by When

It's been said that a goal is a dream with a deadline. Although that sounds nice, it's only half right. Goals aren't dreams. Dreams are barely remembered and often unrealistic. But goals have a deadline. Goals are clearly defined, clearly timed, and clearly achieved.

There is one question that you must ask to use your Purpose Factor every day: "What by when?"

Let's deconstruct the question. The "what" is the goal that will bring you closer to using your purpose. What must you do to use your Purpose Factor? The "when" is the measurement of time. It could be today, in the next six months, or the next decade.

<u>What</u> do I need to do <u>today</u> that brings me closer to using my Purpose Factor?

What do I need to do this month that brings me closer to using my Purpose Factor?

What do I need to do this year that brings me closer to using my Purpose Factor?

Asking "What by when" is the clarifying question you need to evaluate what you do and what you're working towards.

A fulfilled life is made of fulfilled decades. A fulfilled decade is made of fulfilled years. And fulfilled years are made of fulfilled months complete with fulfilled days. You will never live the life you want to live without connecting your days, weeks, months, and years to your Purpose Factor. In his book, *The Long View*, Matthew Kelly writes, "Most people overestimate what they can do in a day, and underestimate what they can do in a month. We overestimate what we can do in a year, and underestimate what we can accomplish in a decade." If you want to use your Purpose Factor to live a great life, it starts by taking an account of your goals and asking, "What by when?"

Setting Better Goals

Andrew Carnegie said, "If you want to be happy, set a goal that commands your thoughts, liberates your energy, and inspires your hopes." Connect your goal to your purpose and you won't only be happy. You'll be fulfilled. In this section of the book, we break down your current goals, help you set Purpose Factor goals, and create a process to evaluate future opportunities.

1. Evaluate Your Current Goals

What are your current goals? You may have a specific goal, like increasing your sales numbers next year or launching a podcast. Maybe you don't have a specific goal—you just want to get through this next season. Or perhaps you wouldn't call it a goal, but there are things that you want to do: you've always wanted to write a book, you've thought about starting a company, or you want to train for a marathon. No matter what you are working towards, you must determine whether it aligns with who you are and who you can help.

Now that you know your Purpose Factor and the clarifying question, you can use both of them to evaluate your goals. Make a list of your goals in your journal. They could be small goals you plan on doing this week. They could be big goals that take a lifetime to achieve. They can be silly. They can be serious. Write them down, all of them.

Now, take each goal, one by one, and ask yourself the clarifying question: *Is this getting me closer to or further away from using my Purpose Factor?*

Next, you will do one of two things: delete it or reframe it. We reframe goals that get us closer to using our Purpose Factor. We delete goals that take us further from using our Purpose Factor.

Perhaps your goal was to get your master's degree. Now with your Purpose Factor in hand, you reevaluate the goal and determine it doesn't get you closer to your purpose. That goal was made because you didn't think you had the authority to do what you do. For you, getting a degree doesn't make you more capable of using your Purpose Factor to help others. This is a goal that you delete.

Maybe the goal is good, but it needs to be reframed. After asking the clarifying question, you determine the goal is helping you get closer to your purpose. Now, you must reframe the goal by connecting it directly to your Purpose Factor. Before he was a best-selling author, Bishop T.D. Jakes used the $15,000 he and his wife saved for a down payment on a house to pay for the printing of his first book. His original goal was to save up enough money for a house, but when he came face to face with his Purpose Factor, he reframed the goal. He used that money to print five thousand copies that he sold out of in two weeks. That book sold over five million copies and is translated in ten different languages. Purpose Factor goals have powerful results.

Evaluate your current goals then establish new goals that are directly aligned with your Purpose Factor.

2. Establish Purpose Factor Goals

You now know who you are and who you can help. You have everything you need to use your Purpose Factor every day. You can use it at work, use it at home, and use it in your community. But here's the key: you have to have a plan on how you will use your Purpose Factor. That plan is made by setting goals.

Your goals should be made by asking a version of the clarifying question: **What can I do that will bring me closer to using my Purpose Factor? When must I do it by?**

In other words, "What by when?"

When you don't know what kind of goals to set, use the same paradigm as the five areas of habits: faith, family, finance, health, and work. These areas are specific enough to give you a framework to start with and general enough to give you the freedom to make them yours.

To prove the point, let's focus on the area of finance. Your goal is to get out of credit card debt. You have determined this will help you get closer to using your Purpose Factor because you will have more money and time to use what you have to help others. Next, ask the clarifying question.

What can I do with my finances that will bring me closer to using my Purpose Factor? Your answer is cutting unnecessary expenses and getting a second income source to pay your debt off faster. Next, ask the second part of the question.

When must I cut expenses and get a second income source by? That answer then becomes part of your goal. It becomes your "What by when."

We have a list of "What by whens" in every area of our life. How much we want to have invested by when. How much we want to grow our team by when. How much we want to go on vacation by when. No matter where you are in your life, the power of "What by when" will work for you.

The entire question is game-changing, but the second part of the question is perhaps the most powerful. Just saying that you have a goal will not make it happen, but attaching a deadline to it will. The truth is, our ability to effectively use our Purpose Factor will depend on how we set and achieve goals.

To set Purpose Factor goals, you must connect the right goals to the right timeline for the right reasons.

3. Evaluate New Opportunities

When someone comes to you with a new opportunity that sounds good, you want to say yes. Yes to the job offer. Yes to the board position. Yes to volunteering on weekends. Yes to the free doughnut.

Most of us do. But the most fulfilled people know that using your purpose means saying no, more than yes. They say no to other people's agendas. They say no to what will become a distraction, things that sound good but will ultimately take them off track from using their Purpose Factor to help others. Notice that the definition of Purpose Factor is "what you have to help others." It is not "what other people want you to do for them."

Your purpose comes from the inside and goes out to help others. It doesn't start with what other people think you should do for them. But sometimes the two can seem confusing.

Let's say you get a new job offer out of the blue. The pay is much more than you make now, but you would have to move out of the country. You ask yourself the clarifying question: **Does this get me closer to or further away from using my Purpose Factor?** For you, the answer isn't exactly clear. You can make the connection, but it's a fuzzy one.

When we have an opportunity that doesn't directly connect to our purpose, we have a "one-degree" rule. Our rule is simple: if we can connect the opportunity to our purpose by one degree of separation, then we will consider it. Notice we didn't say we would do it. We would *consider* it. One degree could be anything. It could be time. For example, an opportunity may not connect to our purpose now, but in six months it could directly support it. A degree could be a connection. The job may not let you use every element of your Purpose Factor, but with the right introduction, it could be a game-changer. A degree could be more education or even more influence. In other words, don't say no to everything if you don't see an immediate connection to your Purpose Factor. However, don't say yes to everything only because it could *maybe* support your Purpose Factor.

We created the one-degree rule because we had to. We would come across new opportunities and get distracted by the possibilities. We justified decisions, moves, partnerships, and investments because of how they *could* connect to our purpose. We had elaborate plans that took too many steps to connect our Purpose Factor to the opportunity. It was all based on potential possibilities and hair-brained happenstance. They never turned into what we wanted because we weren't asking ourselves the question: Does this get me closer to or further away from using my Purpose Factor?

The one-degree rule works because it simplifies decision-making. Pick the opportunities that are most aligned with your purpose, and ditch the ones that will take you off course. If you do not evaluate opportunities through the one-degree rule, you will find yourself saying yes to everyone and no to your purpose.

Your Purpose Factor is your priority. Anything that does not support your purpose does not belong on your agenda.

Using Your Purpose Factor Today

There is a simple solution to the question "How do I use my Purpose Factor today?" Go back to the sequence: people, problem, solution.

Start with "who"? After you ask yourself, "Who will you help today?" you can then determine your "what"—the problem you can uniquely help them solve. The problem you can solve for them will determine the solution that you can specifically give to them. People, problem, solution.

If you are going to work, you can use the Purpose Factor. Start with the right questions: Who can I help with my Purpose Factor today? Is it your coworkers, your boss, or your customers? Who you are serving will determine the problem you solve for them and the solution that you provide.

To find out how to use your Purpose Factor at home, start with the same question: Who can I help with my Purpose Factor today? Is it your kids? Is it your spouse? Is it your parents? Determine your "who," and the problem and solution fall into place.

You can also use your Purpose Factor in the community by using the same question: Who can I help with my Purpose Factor today? Who can you help with what you have inside of you? Is it a nonprofit? A local school? A group of voters? Your neighbor who has cancer? Purpose is not confined to employment. Some of the most purposeful people we know do not have traditional jobs. They are retired generals that teach leadership to young professionals. They are homeschooling moms. They live in mansions and convalescent homes. They are men and women who decide to use what they have to help others no matter where they are.

Every element of your Purpose Factor, from discovering it to using it, starts with "who."

Does Purpose Change?

When we teach the Purpose Factor process, we are often asked, "Does your purpose change, or is it the same your whole life?"

It's a great question, and one of our favorites to hear. The answer: no, your purpose does not change. What changes are the people you serve, the problem you solve, and the solution that you provide.

For example, your Purpose Factor may be a Builder + Messenger + Problem Solver + Trauma Overcomer. That does not change throughout your life. That is what has made you, built you, and shaped your perspective. What does change is how you use your Purpose Factor and who you help with your Purpose Factor.

Maybe in your twenties you get a job in communications. You use your Purpose Factor, specifically your Trauma Overcomer story, to help coworkers feel safe at work. Perhaps in your thirties, you start a company and use your Purpose Factor to consult companies on harassment and creating respectful workplaces. During your thirties and forties, you have children and decide to stay home to raise them. Now you use your Purpose Factor to help raise awareness for sexual harassment in the community, at your kids' schools, and through your online blog.

Your Purpose Factor is the lens that you use to see the world. You don't leave your Purpose Factor at the door when you walk into work. You don't forget it when you become a parent. Your purpose does not retire when you retire. Your purpose is yours to use in every situation and at every stage in your life. Purpose is vocation agnostic.

20

Your Purpose Is Your Permission

"You need to find your purpose" may sound like throwaway advice. But finding your Purpose Factor, as you have learned, will change everything.

No matter your age, your experience, or your mistakes, you have everything inside of you to live out your Purpose Factor. You know the people you were made to help, the problem you were designed to solve, and the solution you are prepared to deliver. You know that you cannot help others with your purpose without first finding your purpose. You now understand what will hold you back from finding your purpose—the bad beliefs, the comparison, the mindsets—that steal your fulfillment and your impact. You have replaced the feelings of hopelessness with hope and traded uneasiness for confidence about what's next.

At this point, we want you to do something: we want you to imagine what you will look like when you are living fully in your purpose. Who will you be helping? How will you be living? What will your average day look like?

Now stop. How easily did that picture come to you? Did you have a hard time coming up with something specific, or was the picture bright and clear? The more you focus on using your Purpose Factor, the clearer and the closer that picture becomes.

We want to share with you how to transform yourself into the picture you have in your head. Take your journal back out and write down what is holding you back. It could be your finances, a lack of support at home, or the opportunities that don't seem to work out. It could be big things or small things; write them all down. Now, looking at that list, we want to ask you a question. Are you excited or discouraged about pursuing your purpose? If you're like most people, you feel like you've shrunk a few inches. That's because even by writing them down, you have given those things power over your purpose. It's time to take that power back.

So do this. One by one, scratch out the reasons that you can't live out your purpose. Better yet, get a black Sharpie pen and put a big "X" over them.

Why do this? When you label your excuses and scratch them out, it gives your brain permission to scratch them from your belief system. When you believe that life is limiting, it will limit you. When you believe that life is full of opportunities, doors will open to you. When you believe that you have permission, you won't wait for permission. It's only when you eliminate what has held you back in the past that you can run—not walk—into the life you imagined.

Permission Granted

"You have permission to pursue your purpose."

We didn't know it then, but that phrase would become the most powerful moment of our three days together.

We held our first Purpose Factor retreat in a beautiful mansion in Charlottesville, Virginia. The participants signed up for a weekend to find their purpose but didn't know much else. As we led each individual through the simple process of finding their Purpose Factor, we saw glimpses of transformation.

Lies that they couldn't shake were being rewritten with the truth about who they were. Doubt was being replaced by courage. Confusion was being erased as clarity took over for these ten individuals. It's like the light had finally come on.

As we wrapped up the weekend, everyone stood in the main hall with their Purpose Factor scribbled down in their notebooks. We hugged them one by one, and as we did, we told them, "Your purpose *is* your permission."

From that moment, they were fully transformed. They didn't need to wait for someone else to give them permission to live out their purpose. They didn't need to worry if their ambition or confidence made other people feel uncomfortable.

Their purpose was their permission.

Humans are hardwired to ask for permission. As children, we ask if we can have a snack. As teenagers, we test boundaries around what is and what is not acceptable. And as adults, we look to others to say it is okay for us to achieve and advance.

Through our study of permission, we have found that most of us seek permission from one of four groups: parents, partners, experts, and experience. We seek permission from parents when we are young, and even into our early adulthood. We do not want to disappoint the people who raised us, so we study subjects they like, take jobs they want, and marry people they approve of. In the same way, we seek permission from our partners. We don't want to disrupt our partner's view of us if we fail. We also don't want to inject instability into the relationship—especially if things are already rocky. This causes us to stay in jobs we hate and put off pursuing our purpose.

We don't just seek permission from people we know. We also look to experts to give us permission. The expert could be an educational institution, a certification, or a respected person in the industry. We think, "If I just get them to say I have what it takes, I will do it." We think more education, more certificates, and more awards will make us more worthy of pursuing our purpose. But it won't.

Finally, we seek permission from experience. "I couldn't possibly do that, I don't have enough experience" is a common objection we hear. And so we wait for years and years, thinking one day we will be accomplished enough or practiced enough to deserve to be fulfilled. But that day will never come unless you transform your mindset about where permission comes from.

Speed Bumps and Fences

Every time we seek permission from others, we put our purpose in someone else's hands. Usually, those hands don't know or don't understand our purpose.

A friend of ours sold his first company before he turned thirty. It was a large tech company that he and his team had built from the ground up. His mother didn't understand what he did and was outspoken about her disapproval of his career choice. She would ask him, "Why don't you move home and get a job here?"

If our friend had waited for permission from his mom to start his company, it never would have happened. If he would have sought her approval above pursuing his purpose, he would have never experienced fulfillment. After the deal finalized, our friend called his mom to tell her that he had sold the company. "How much did you get for it?" she asked. When he responded with a massive number, her response was "Oh, that's it?"

Those you seek permission from may never give it to you. **The truth is that you have to be more afraid of living outside of your purpose than what others think of you.** You have to let go of the fear of failing, fear of rejection, and the fear of not being understood. It's the only way that you can fully be who you are meant to be. You have to be willing to walk alone—at least until you find a community that will build you up and support you.

Even when you are fully living your Purpose Factor, people will question you. You may have a spouse who loves you but cannot see your purpose because they don't know their own. You may have parents who cherish you but cannot see your purpose because they are lost in their own struggles.

There are two types of people who will stand in your way. Those who actively stand against your purpose and those who passively stand against your purpose. We call the ones who actively try to stop you "fences," and the ones who passively don't support you the "speed bumps." The fences will try and hold you back. They will act out when you need their support. They will mock you when you start to act differently. They will sabotage your efforts moving forward. Fences make it seem like there is no way around them—but there is always a way. If you are determined enough, no fence will stop you. Unlike the *fences*, the *speed bumps* don't try to stand in your way. However, they don't help you either. Speed bumps slow your momentum. They may ask questions at first, skeptical to see if you will actually follow through with what you say. In either case, those who do not support your purpose do it for the same reason: they don't know their own Purpose Factor (and maybe they need this book).

It can be heartbreaking to see those you love not supporting your purpose. But it is more heartbreaking to know your purpose and never use it.

The Future, Now

You have just gone on the journey of discovering your Purpose Factor. This is what less than 1 percent of people are willing or know how to do. Don't put your breakthrough in the drawer. Don't hide who you are. Don't put off using it.

If you discover your purpose and don't use it, one thing will happen. You will be bitter. That bitterness will replace any sense of clarity and breakthrough that you have experienced thus far. It will seep into your relationships. You will blame others and yourself for not letting yourself be who you really are. But if you give yourself permission to use your Purpose Factor, you will be open to endless opportunities.

As we have discussed, your Purpose Factor does not change over your lifetime. The people you help will change. The way you help them may change. Even the scope of how you help people may change. We see living out your Purpose Factor like chiseling a sculpture out of a block of marble. You get to decide how it is going to turn out. The more focused your work, the more detailed the statue. The more time you spend on it, the more exquisite it will turn out. You can't hack off a corner of marble and call it a sculpture. You can't find your purpose in a few minutes and call it a day. They both take time.

We designed the Purpose Factor as a process on purpose (pun intended). We knew that if we just spit out your Purpose like a vending machine, it wouldn't mean much to you. Why? Because as humans, we cherish what we work for. Uncovering your Purpose Factor took some time. It required reflection. We asked you to expose your deepest dreams, your true identity, and the things that most break your heart. They have become the tools in your hand. It's now up to you to use them.

Perhaps the easiest way we can explain how to use your Purpose Factor is a children's song turned civil rights anthem.

"This Little Light of Mine" was first written in the 1920s as a song for children. It grew in popularity, appearing in movies and pop music for nearly a century, and became the anthem for the civil rights movement in the 1960s. Its simple lyrics send a powerful message.

This little light of mine,
Yes, I'm gonna let it shine.
Let it shine, let it shine, let it shine.
The light that shines is the light of love,
Lights the darkness from above.
It shines on you and it shines on me,
and it shows what the light of love can do.
I'm gonna shine my light both far and near,
I'm gonna shine my light bright and clear.
Where there's a dark corner in this land
I'm gonna let my little light shine.

We first heard this song as children. It doesn't seem profound until you look at it through the lens of your Purpose Factor. We all have a light inside of us. It is up to us how bright we will let it shine. We dim the light when we ask for permission from others. It starts to flicker when we set unrealistic expectations for ourselves. It is barely given a chance to burn when we keep harmful habits alive. But when guarded and grown, the light we have inside has the capacity to grow into a flame. It starts as a soft glow, then grows to a burn, and then all at once, it's ablaze. The more we fan the flame of our purpose, the more people we help and the more fulfilled we feel.

Our Purpose Factor shines like the light inside of us. Just as the light in this children's song helps others, our Purpose Factor is not for ourselves. Light exposes darkness. It helps others see clearly. It shows the beauty that was once hidden. It has a purpose.

You must use the light for yourself before you can use it to help others. When you know who you are and who you are here to help, everything falls into place.

You already know the answer to the question “Who am I?” With your Purpose Factor in hand, the only question to answer is simple. “Who can I now help?”

About the Authors

Brian Bosché

Brian is the CEO and co-founder of The Purpose Company. He is a former national journalist, bestselling author, and international speaker. Brian and his team at The Purpose Company help companies and individuals find their purpose and use it to experience maximum fulfillment. He has worked with Fortune 500 companies, the U.S. Air Force, and A-list celebrities, and designed strategies for leaders looking to lead and work on purpose. Brian has co-hosted SiriusXM programming and has appeared on NPR, *The Economist*, and Fox News Channel.

For booking: PurposeCompany.co

Gabrielle Bosché

Gabrielle is the co-founder of The Purpose Company. She is one of the most requested speakers on generational leadership in the world, a bestselling author, and popular TEDx presenter. Gabrielle has personally worked with the U.S. military, Fortune 500 companies, and presidential campaigns. Gabrielle has co-hosted SiriusXM programming and been featured on NPR, *Glamour*, *Fast Company*, Business Insider, and Bloomberg Radio.

For booking: PurposeCompany.co

A POST HILL PRESS BOOK

The Purpose Factor:
Extreme Clarity for Why You're Here And What to Do About It

ISBN: 978-1-64293-493-9
ISBN (eBook): 978-1-64293-494-6

Interior design and composition, Greg Johnson, Textbook Perfect

Post Hill Press
New York • Nashville
posthillpress.com
Published in the United States of America

Want Your Purpose Factor Story Featured?

PurposeFactorBook.com/story

References by Chapter

CHAPTER 1: YOUR PURPOSE FACTOR

1. **Japanese Television Show Exploring Longevity and "Ikigai"**

   Dayman, Lucy. "Ikigai: The Japanese Concept of Finding Purpose in Life." Savvy Tokyo, January 15, 2020. https://savvy-tokyo.com/ikigai-japanese-concept-finding-purpose-life/.

CHAPTER 2: FIGURING OUT WHAT'S NEXT

1. **Oprah Winfrey's Quote about Finding Your Purpose**

   Winfrey, Oprah. "Ask Oprah: How Did You Discover Your Purpose?" National Museum of African American History and Culture, June 8, 2018. YouTube video. https://www.youtube.com/watch?v=fAz9qLTC4EY.

2. **Oprah Winfrey's Story**

   Harris, Paul. "You Go, Girl." *Guardian*, November 19, 2005. https://www.theguardian.com/media/2005/nov/20/television.usa.

3. **Dwayne "The Rock" Johnson's Story**

   "Dwayne Johnson." *Empire*. Accessed February 27, 2020. https://www.empireonline.com/people/dwayne-johnson/.

Gadot, Gal. "TIME 100: Dwayne 'the Rock' Johnson." *Time*, April 16, 2019. https://time.com/time_tout/dwayne-johnson-time-100/.

Johnson, Dwayne. "Seven Bucks Moment: Dwayne 'The Rock' Johnson." The Rock, December 6, 2016. YouTube video. https://www.youtube.com/watch?v=RjATMi9yNdo.

Mejia, Zameena. "How Dwayne 'the Rock' Johnson Went from Evictions and Struggle to Making $89 Million a Year." CNBC, June 6, 2018. https://www.cnbc.com/2018/06/06/the-rock-went-from-evictions-to-making-65-million-a-year.html.

Winfrey, Oprah. "What Dwayne Johnson Learned after Being Booed by 20,000 Wrestling Fans." Oprah.com, November 15, 2015. Video. http://www.oprah.com/own-master-class/what-dwayne-johnson-learned-after-being-booed-by-20000-fans-video.

4. **Sheryl Sandberg's Story**

Dixon, Brandon J. "Leaning in from Harvard Yard to Facebook: Sheryl K. Sandberg '91." *Harvard Crimson*, May 24, 2016. https://www.thecrimson.com/article/2016/5/24/Sheryl-Sandberg-profile/.

Leskin, Paige. "The Career Rise and Life of Sheryl Sandberg, Facebook's Billionaire Chief Operating Officer Who Just Announced She's Engaged." *Business Insider*, February 3, 2020. https://www.businessinsider.com/fabulous-life-of-sheryl-sandberg-2014-7.

5. **Billie Jean King's Story**

"American Masters: Billie Jean King." PBS, September 10, 2013. https://www.pbs.org/wnet/americanmasters/billie-jean-king-film-billie-jean-king/2637/.

6. **Nelson Mandela's Story**

Vallely, Paul. "A Life in Focus: Nelson Mandela, 'Trouble-maker' Who Became the Father of South African Democracy." *Independent,* July 24, 2018. https://www.independent.co.uk/news/lifeinfocus/nelson-mandela-apartheid-south-africa-life-in-focus-book-nobel-prize-a8457181.html.

7. **Titan Gilroy's Story**

Hitch, John. "The Fall and Rise of an Industrial Icon." New Equipment Digest, February 9, 2018. https://www.newequipment.com/industry-trends/article/22059709/the-fall-and-rise-of-an-industrial-icon.

8. **Sir Richard Branson's Story**

Branson, Richard. "How I Started Seven Different Businesses as a Teenager," Virgin, February 9, 2017. https://www.virgin.com/richard-branson/how-i-started-seven-different-businesses-teenager.

Norris, Emily. "How Did Richard Branson Make His Fortune?" Investopedia, January 27, 2020. https://www.investopedia.com/ask/answers/032615/how-did-richard-branson-make-his-fortune.asp.

Schwartz, Emily K. "Richard Branson and the Dyslexia Advantage." *Washington Post*, November 7, 2012. https://www.washingtonpost.com/national/on-innovations/richard-branson-and-the-dyslexia-advantage/2012/11/07/67a05b2a-2906-11e2-bab2-eda299503684_story.html.

9. **Jeff Bezos's Story**

Clifford, Catherine. "What Jeff Bezos Learned about How to Be Successful Working on His Grandfather's Ranch as a Kid." CNBC, May 14, 2018. https://www.cnbc.com/2018/05/14/what-jeff-bezos-learned-about-how-to-be-successful-working-on-his-grandfathers-ranch-as-a-kid.html.

"Family of Voices: Miguel Bezos." National Museum of American History. Smithsonian Institution, July 31, 2017. https://americanhistory.si.edu/family-voices/individuals/miguel-bezos.

Mark, Gina. "20 Things about Jeff Bezos You Probably Didn't Know." *People* (blog). Hongkiat.com, August 3, 2018. https://www.hongkiat.com/blog/amazon-jeff-bezos/.

Martin, Emmie. "Jeff Bezos Hasn't Always Had the Golden Touch: Here's What the Amazon Founder Was Doing in His 20s." CNBC, August 2, 2017. https://www.cnbc.com/2017/08/02/what-amazon-billionaire-jeff-bezos-was-doing-in-his-20s.html.

CHAPTER 3: THE PURSUIT TO MATTER

1. **The Dialogue from the Movie** ***The Wedding Date***

The Wedding Date. Directed by Clare Kilner. Written by Elizabeth Young (book) and Dana Fox (screenplay). Beverly Hills: Gold Circle Films, 2005. DVD.

2. **The Definition of the Word "Potential"**

Lexico.com. Oxford University Press. S.v. "potential." Accessed February 27, 2020. https://www.lexico.com/en/definition/potential.

CHAPTER 4: SETTING BIG GOALS

1. **Statistic on Percentage of Americans That Make New Year's Resolutions**

   Shapiro, Stephen. "There Is No Correlation between Happiness and Resolution Setting." Inc.com, December 27, 2018. https://www.inc.com/stephen-shapiro/92-of-people-fail-to-achieve-their-new-years-resolutions.html.

2. **Australian Study on Why People Fail to Keep Their New Year's Resolutions**

   "Be a Geek and Live in Tasmania: How to Win at New Year's Resolutions." Finder AU, December 9, 2015. https://www.finder.com.au/press-release-new-years-resolution-statistics-2015-2016.

3. **The 1953 Yale University Study on Goal Setting That Never Happened**

   Tabak, Lawrence. "If Your Goal Is Success, Don't Consult These Gurus." *Fast Company*, December 31, 1996. https://www.fastcompany.com/27953/if-your-goal-success-dont-consult-these-gurus.

4. **Story about Dale Hammock Wondering What to Do after Release from Prison**

   Mooallem, Jon. "You Just Got out of Prison. Now What?" *New York Times*, July 16, 2015. https://www.nytimes.com/2015/07/19/magazine/you-just-got-out-of-prison-now-what.html.

CHAPTER 5: PURSUING PASSION

1. **The Dialogue from the Movie *Talladega Nights: The Ballad of Ricky Bobby***

   Talladega Nights: The Ballad of Ricky Bobby. Directed by Adam McKay. Written by Will Ferrell and Adam McKay. Culver City, CA: Sony Pictures Entertainment, 2006. DVD.

2. **The Definition of the Word "Passion"**

   Lexico. Oxford University Press. S.v. "passion." Accessed February 27, 2020. https://www.lexico.com/en/definition/passion.

3. **Quotes about Passion with Attribution**

   "Always go with your passions. Never ask yourself if it's realistic or not." *—Deepak Chopra*

   "Dreams and passion are more powerful than facts and reality." *—Shubam Shaw*

   "No alarm clock needed. My passion wakes me." *—Kyrie Irving*

   "Turn your passion into your paycheck." *—Unknown*

4. **Smithsonian Study on Number of People Majoring in History**

   Daley, Jason. "Why Are Fewer People Majoring in History?" *Smithsonian Magazine*, November 29, 2018. https://www.smithsonianmag.com/smart-news/why-people-major-history-180970913/.

5. **Study on Whether Passion Is Fixed or Grows over Time**

O'Keefe, Paul A., Carol S. Dweck, and Gregory M. Walton. "Implicit Theories of Interest: Finding Your Passion or Developing It?" *Psychological Science* 29, no. 10 (2018): 1653–1664.

6. **Mike Rowe on the Folly of Following Your Passion**

Rowe, Mike. "Don't Follow Your Passion." PragerU, June 6, 2016. YouTube video. https://www.youtube.com/watch?v=CVEuPmVAb8o.

7. **Quote from Steve Jobs's 2005 Stanford University Commencement Address**

Jobs, Steve and John Hennessy. "Steve Jobs' 2005 Stanford Commencement Address." Stanford University, May 14, 2008. YouTube video. https://www.youtube.com/watch?v=Hd_ptbiPoXM.

8. **Cal Newport's Book, *So Good They Can't Ignore You***

Newport, Cal. *So Good They Can't Ignore You: Why Skills Trump Passion in the Quest for Work You Love.* New York: Grand Central Publishing, 2012.

CHAPTER 6: FULFILLING MY DUTIES

1. **Story about Suzanne Watson Going to Medical School in Her 50s**

Watson, Suzanne. "Changing Channels: Millions of Women Wait Years to Fulfill Their Dreams—or to Figure out What Their Dreams Are. Here Are Some of Their Stories." *Washington Post*, June 9, 2019. https://www.washingtonpost.com/graphics/2019/lifestyle/women-over-50/.

2. **Letter to the Editor by Ruth Wibking, R.N. in the September 1972 Edition of the** ***American Journal of Nursing***

Wibking, Ruth H. "Majority of Nurses Suffer from Martyr Syndrome." *American Journal of Nursing* 72, no. 9 (September 1972).

3. **Study by Emma Reinhardt on Martyr Complex in Teachers**

Reinhardt, Emma. "A Martyr Complex." *The Clearing House: A Journal of Educational Strategies, Issues and Ideas* 31 (1957).

4. **Study on Children of Working Moms**

McGinn, Kathleen L., Mayra Ruiz Castro, and Elizabeth Long Lingo. "Learning from Mum: Cross-National Evidence Linking Maternal Employment and Adult Children's Outcomes." *Work, Employment and Society* 33, no. 3 (2019): 374–400.

5. **Quote by Kathleen L. McGinn, Ph.D., Reflecting on the Study about Children of Working Moms**

Gerdeman, Dina. "Kids of Working Moms Grow into Happy Adults." Harvard Business School Working Knowledge, July 16, 2018. https://hbswk.hbs.edu/item/kids-of-working-moms-grow-into-happy-adults.

CHAPTER 7: FINDING HAPPINESS

1. **The Eighteenth-Century Fable about Prince Rasselas**

Johnson, Samuel. *The Prince of Abissinia: A Tale.* Oxford: Clarendon Press, 1759.

2. **A Perspective on Happiness by Aristotle**

Aristotle. *Aristotle in 23 Volumes*. Vol. 19. *Nicomachean Ethics*. Translated by H. Rackham. London: William Heinemann Ltd. 1934. 1098a16.

3. **Author and Neuroscientist Dean Burnett's Perspective on Happiness**

Fox, Killian. "Dean Burnett: 'Happiness Shouldn't Be the Default State in the Human Brain.' " *Guardian*, April 28, 2018. https://www.theguardian.com/books/2018/apr/28/dean-burnett-happiness-should-not-default-state-human-brain-the-happy-brain.

4. **Study on Whether Prioritizing Happiness Makes You More or Less Happy**

Mauss, Iris B., Maya Tamir, Craig L. Anderson, and Nicole S. Savino. "Can Seeking Happiness Make People Unhappy? Paradoxical Effects of Valuing Happiness." *Emotion* 11, no. 4 (2011): 807.

5. **Study on Students Interested in Learning Photography and Happiness**

Gilbert, Daniel T., and Jane EJ Ebert. "Decisions and Revisions: The Affective Forecasting of Changeable Outcomes." *Journal of Personality and Social Psychology* 82, no. 4 (2002): 503.

6. **Study on How Spending Money on Others Promotes Happiness**

Dunn, Elizabeth W., Lara B. Aknin, and Michael I. Norton. "Spending Money on Others Promotes Happiness." *Science* 319, no. 5870 (2008): 1687–1688.

7. **Nancy Nall's Blog on Tim Goeglein's Plagiarism**

Nall, Nancy. "Copycat." *NancyNall.com* (blog), February 29, 2008. http://nancynall.com/2008/02/29/copycat/.

CHAPTER 8: THE OXYGEN MASK PRINCIPLE

1. **The Dialogue from the Movie *Fight Club***

   Fight Club. Directed by David Fincher. Written by Chuck Palahniuk (book) and Jim Uhls (screenplay). Los Angeles: Fox 2000 Pictures, 1999. DVD.

2. **Tracey Bryan's Story about Experiencing Hypoxia on a Royal Australian Air Force Flight**

   Bryan, Tracey. Reply to "In What Scenarios Have Oxygen Masks Actually Been Necessary on an Airplane?" Quora, December 29, 2013. https://www.quora.com/In-what-scenarios-have-oxygen-masks-actually-been-necessary-on-an-airplane.

3. **Ancient Principle about the Speck in Your Neighbor's Eye**

   Matthew 7:3–5 (ESV).

4. **Statistics about the Size and Scope of the Self-Help Industry**

   LaRosa, John. "What's Next for the $9.9 Billion Personal Development Industry." *Market Research Blog*. Market-Research.com, January 17, 2018. https://blog.marketresearch.com/whats-next-for-the-9-9-billion-personal-development-industry.

5. **Study on Nurse Mortality**

   Gu, Fangyi, Jiali Han, Francine Laden, An Pan, Neil E. Caporaso, Meir J. Stampfer, Ichiro Kawachi et al. "Total and Cause-Specific Mortality of US Nurses Working Rotating Night Shifts." *American Journal of Preventive Medicine* 48, no. 3 (2015): 241–252.

6. **Study on Acting Yourself into Higher Self-Esteem**

Pillemer, David, Kristina Steiner, and Dorthe Kirkegaard Thomsen. "Writing about Life Story Chapters Increases Self Esteem: Three Experimental Studies." *Journal of Personality* 87, no. 5 (Fall 2018): 962–980.

CHAPTER 9: CHOOSE YOUR CRISIS BEFORE YOUR CRISIS CHOOSES YOU

1. **Story about Alex Trebek's Pancreatic Cancer Diagnosis**

Rivas, Anthony and Ann Reynolds. " 'Jeopardy!' Host Alex Trebek on Outpouring of Support for Cancer Battle: 'My Gosh, It Makes Me Feel So Good.' " ABC News, December 30, 2019. https://abcnews.go.com/Entertainment/jeopardy-host-alex-trebek-outpouring-support-cancer-battle/story?id=67765903.

2. **Statistics on Number of Television Hours Watched by American Adults in 2016**

Koblin, John. "How Much Do We Love TV? Let Us Count the Ways." *New York Times*, June 30, 2016. https://www.nytimes.com/2016/07/01/business/media/nielsen-survey-media-viewing.html.

3. **Study on Control over and Perception of Physical Pain**

Beck, Brianna, Steven Di Costa, and Patrick Haggard. "Having Control over the External World Increases the Implicit Sense of Agency." *Cognition* 162 (2017): 54–60.

4. **Tom Bilyeu's Interview with Former Drug Addict Doug Bopst**

Bopst, Doug. "Doug Bopst: Former Drug Addict Explains How to Completely Turn Your Life Around." Interview by Tom Bilyeu. Impact Theory, August 5, 2019. https://impacttheory.com/episode/doug-bopst/.

5. **Continued Story about Alex Trebek's Pancreatic Cancer Diagnosis**

Rivas and Reynolds, " 'Jeopardy!' Host Alex Trebek."

CHAPTER 10: COMPARISON KILLS PURPOSE

1. **Story about the Fake German Heiress Anna Delvey**

Allen, Jonathan. "Fake Heiress Who Dazzled New York Elite Gets 4 to 12 Years for Fraud." Reuters, May 9, 2019. https://www.reuters.com/article/us-new-york-crime-fake-heiress/fake-heiress-who-dazzled-new-york-elite-gets-4-to-12-years-for-fraud-idUSKCN1SF236.

Mustian, Jim. "NY Jury Hears Conflicting Portrayals of Fake German Heiress." AP News, April 23, 2019. https://apnews.com/af246aa81f594329b1649508a47c4fa4.

Palmer, Emily, and Jan Ransom. "Fake Heiress Who Swindled N.Y.'s Elite Is Found Guilty." *New York Times*, April 25, 2019. https://www.nytimes.com/2019/04/25/nyregion/anna-delvey-sorokin-verdict.html.

2. **Study on the Consequences of Social Comparison**

Salovey, Peter, and Judith Rodin. "Some Antecedents and Consequences of Social-Comparison Jealousy." *Journal of Personality and Social Psychology* 47, no. 4 (1984): 780.

3. **Dialogue from the Book *The Great Gatsby***

Fitzgerald, F. Scott. *The Great Gatsby*. New York: Charles Scribner's Sons, 1925.

4. **Mallory Knight's Story about Being Stuck in a Comparison Trap**

Knight, Mallory. "I Was Stuck in a Comparison Trap." *Stories* (blog). NewSpring Church, October 22, 2017. https://newspring.cc/stories/mallory-knight.

5. **Dove Beauty Commercial**

"Dove Real Beauty Sketches | You're More Beautiful Than You Think." Dove US, April 14, 2013. YouTube video. https://www.youtube.com/watch?v=XpaOjMXyJGk.

6. **Story about the 200-Meter Butterfly Race between Michael Phelps and Chad le Clos in 2016**

Zaccardi, Nick. "Chad le Clos Still Has Nightmares of Losing to Michael Phelps in Rio." NBC Sports, February 20, 2017. https://olympics.nbcsports.com/2017/02/20/chad-le-clos-michael-phelps/.

7. **Quote from Michael Phelps Regarding Race Against Chad le Clos**

Lang, Cady "A Guide to Why the Internet Is Losing It Over Michael Phelps Beating Chad le Clos." *Time*, August 10, 2016. https://time.com/4446837/rio-2016-olympics-michael-phelps-chad-le-clos/.

CHAPTER 11: YOUR NATURAL ADVANTAGE

1. **Quote from Anne Lamott's Book, *Bird by Bird***

   Lamott, Anne. *Bird by Bird: Some Instructions on Writing and Life*. 1st ed. New York: Anchor, 1995.

2. **The Dialogue from the Movie *Anger Management***

   Anger Management. Directed by Peter Segal. Written by David Dorfman. Los Angeles: Revolution Studios, 2003. DVD.

CHAPTER 12: YOUR ACQUIRED SKILLS

1. **Warren Buffett's Story**

   Beers, Brian. "What's the First Stock Warren Buffett Ever Bought?" Investopedia, June 25, 2019. https://www.investopedia.com/ask/answers/021915/what-was-first-stock-warren-buffett-ever-bought.asp.

   Encyclopedia Britannica. S.v. "Warren Buffett." August 26, 2019. https://www.britannica.com/biography/Warren-Edward-Buffett.

   "Warren Buffett." *Forbes*, February 28, 2020. https://www.forbes.com/profile/warren-buffett/#308414c74639.

2. **Oprah Winfrey's Story**

   The David Rubenstein Show: Oprah Winfrey. *Bloomberg*, March 1, 2017. Video. https://www.bloomberg.com/news/videos/2017-03-01/the-david-rubenstein-show-oprah-winfrey.

3. **Arnold Schwarzenegger's Story**

   "Arnold Schwarzenegger." Evolution of Bodybuilding, 2018. https://www.evolutionofbodybuilding.net/arnold-schwarzenegger/.

Welsh, Cheryl. "Arnold Schwarzenegger Speaks about the Connection He Had with the Late Award-Winning Actress Lucille Ball: 'I Was Saved.' " Fabiosa, July 31, 2019. https://fabiosa.com/ctclb-rsvlk-aufdg-pbadb-phpvg-arnold-schwarzenegger-speaks-about-the-connection-he-had-with-the-late-award-winning-actress-lucille-ball-i-was-saved/.

4. **Robert Kiyosaki's Story**

   Kiyosaki, Robert. *Rich Dad's before You Quit Your Job: 10 Real-Life Lessons Every Entrepreneur Should Know about Building a Million-Dollar Business.* Scottsdale, AZ: Plata Publishing, 2012.

5. **The Thread for the Reddit Post "My Career Counselor Asked Me This Question"**

   DeliciousGarfield. "My Career Counselor Asked Me This Question." Reddit, August 15, 2019. https://www.reddit.com/r/UofT/comments/cqnaim/my_career_counselor_asked_me_this_question/.

6. **The Story of Ben and Jerry's First Ice Cream Class**

   Martin, Emmie. "The Ben & Jerry's Founders Knew Nothing about Making Ice Cream—So They Took a $5 Class." CNBC, August 1, 2019. https://www.cnbc.com/2019/08/01/ben-and-jerrys-founders-started-out-by-taking-a-5-dollar-ice-cream-class.html.

7. **Steve Jobs's Exploration of Calligraphy**

   Rosoff, Matt. "The Only Reason the Mac Looks like It Does Is Because Steve Jobs Dropped in on a Course Taught by This Former Monk." *Business Insider*, March 8, 2016. https://www.businessinsider.com/robert-palladino-calligraphy-class-inspired-steve-jobs-2016-3.

8. **The Story of Roxanne Quimby and Burt's Bees**

Quimby, Roxanne. "Burt's Bees: Our Story." Burt's Bees. Accessed February 28, 2020. https://www.burtsbees.com/our-story/.

CHAPTER 13: YOUR PULL-PASSION

1. **The Korean Fable "The Story Bag"**

So-Un, Kim. *The Story Bag: A Collection of Korean Folk Tales.* Translated by Setsu Higashi. Rutland, VT: Tuttle Publishing, 1955.

2. **The Definition of the Word "Passion"**

Lexico. Oxford University Press. S.v. "passion." Accessed February 27, 2020. https://www.lexico.com/en/definition/passion.

3. **Jim Carrey's Story and the 10 Million Dollar Check**

"Jim Carrey Manifested His Success." *The Graham Norton Show*, January 28, 2020. Facebook video. https://www.facebook.com/watch/?v=487183095540046.

4. **Surfer Bethany Hamilton's Story**

Hamilton, Bethany. "Learn about Bethany." BethanyHamilton.com. 2020. https://bethanyhamilton.com/biography/.

5. **Leo Tolstoy's Short Story "Where Love Is, God Is"**

Tolstoy, Leo. *Where Love Is, God Is.* Springfield, OH: Crowell Company Publishers, 1887.

CHAPTER 14: YOUR ORIGIN STORY

1. **George Lucas and the Influence of Joseph Campbell's *The Hero with a Thousand Faces***

   Campbell, Joseph. *The Hero with a Thousand Faces.* Novato, CA: New World Library, 2008.

   Linn, Will. "Joseph Campbell Is the Hidden Link between '2001,' 'Star Wars,' and 'Mad Max: Fury Road.'" *IndieWire*, March 12, 2018. https://www.indiewire.com/2018/03/joseph-campbell-heros-journey-2001-star-wars-1201937470/.

2. **Columbia University's Kevin Ochsner on Reframing Negative Moments in Life**

   Konnikova, Maria. "How People Learn to Become Resilient." *New Yorker*, February 11, 2016. https://www.newyorker.com/science/maria-konnikova/the-secret-formula-for-resilience.

3. **Patrik Baboumian's Story**

   Baboumian, Patrik. "What Does It Take to Save the World." TEDx Talks, December 11, 2018. YouTube video. https://www.youtube.com/watch?v=2xoRVIoTOsA.

   Baboumian, Patrik. "Why I Went Vegan." November 28, 2016. YouTube video. https://www.youtube.com/watch?list=PLtc3iQTP5EZ-CpuoVizGtz4Mq2k6iVCxI&time_continue=14&v=k-dk-uOGLAxo&feature=emb_title.

CHAPTER 15: THE PEOPLE YOU WERE MADE TO HELP

1. **The Tumbleweed Tank, Featured in the July 1936 Edition of *Popular Mechanics***

   "The Tumbleweed Tank—Back to the Drawing Board." *Military History Matters*, August 11, 2011. https://www.military-history.org/articles/the-tumbleweed-tank-back-to-the-drawing-board.htm.

2. **Suze Orman's Story about Losing More Than $50,000 of a Friend's Money**

   Orman, Suze. "The Road Not Taken: How Losing $50,000 Became My Biggest Gain." *Suze Orman* (blog), November 18, 2014. https://www.suzeorman.com/blog/the-road-not-taken-how-losing-50000-became-my-biggest-gain.

3. **The Story of Viola Gregg Liuzzo, Civil Rights Martyr**

   "Civil Rights Martyrs." Southern Poverty Law Center, 2020. https://www.splcenter.org/what-we-do/civil-rights-memorial/civil-rights-martyrs.

   "Viola Gregg Liuzzo." Biography.com, February 19, 2016. https://www.biography.com/activist/viola-gregg-liuzzo.

CHAPTER 16: THE PROBLEM YOU WERE DESIGNED TO SOLVE

1. **Sara Blakely and the Moment She Created the First Pair of Spanx**

   Blakely, Sara. "The 'Aha' Moment That Launched Spanx." Inc.com, February 2014. https://www.inc.com/magazine/201402/sara-blakely/spanx-sara-blakely-patent-protection.html.

2. **The Story of William Wilberforce and John Newton**

   "The Creation of 'Amazing Grace.' " Library of Congress. https://www.loc.gov/item/ihas.200149085/.

3. **Discovery Story of Chuck Templeton, Founder of OpenTable**

   Sáles-Griffin, Neal. "Solve a Problem You Care About." *Medium*, April 18, 2014. https://medium.com/@nealsales/solve-a-problem-you-care-about-432bbb5667d1.

CHAPTER 17: THE SOLUTION YOU ARE PREPARED TO DELIVER

1. ***Blue Ocean Strategy* by W. Chan Kim and Renée Mauborgne**

   Kim, W. Chan and Renée Mauborgne. *Blue Ocean Strategy: How to Create Uncontested Market Space and Make Competition Irrelevant*. 1st ed. Boston, MA: Harvard Business Review Press, 2005.

CHAPTER 18: THE LIFE YOU WERE MEANT TO LIVE

1. **Is There Science behind Daily Affirmations?**

   Moore, Catherine. "Positive Daily Affirmations: Is There Science behind It?" PositivePsychology.com, July 4, 2019. https://positivepsychology.com/daily-affirmations/.

CHAPTER 19: SETTING PURPOSE FACTOR GOALS

1. **Matthew Kelly's book, *The Long View***

   Kelly, Matthew. *The Long View: Some Thoughts about One of Life's Most Important Lessons*. Erlanger, KY: Beacon Publishing, 2014.

2. **Bishop T.D. Jakes's Story**

   Jakes, T.D. and Furtick. "How to Build Your Vision from the Ground Up." Elevation Church, October 26, 2017. YouTube video. https://www.youtube.com/watch?v=QVGk_jwyBXI.

CHAPTER 20: YOUR PURPOSE IS YOUR PERMISSION

1. **Lyrics from the Song "This Little Light of Mine"**

   Loes, Harry Dixon. "This Little Light of Mine." 1920.